REAL ESTATE VALUATION

Principles & Practice

Dr. Adv. HARSHUL SAVLA

Ph.D. (MU), MMS (JBIMS), LL.M (MU), LL.B (GLC), BMS (NM)

INDIA • SINGAPORE • MALAYSIA

Notion Press

No.8, 3rd Cross Street,
CIT Colony, Mylapore,
Chennai, Tamil Nadu – 600004

First Published by Notion Press 2021
Copyright © Dr. Adv. Harshul Savla 2021
All Rights Reserved.

ISBN 978-1-63832-587-1

ABOUT THE AUTHOR

Dr. Adv. Harshul Savla (MRICS)

Dr. Adv. Harshul Savla (MRICS) is a Principal Partner of M Realty (Suvidha Lifespaces) which has successfully completed more than 1.2 million sq.ft. in last 30 years across Mumbai City under the able leadership of Mr. Pramesh Rambhiya. CRISIL India recognized Dr. Harshul as "Young Thought Leader" and Realty NXT featured him as "Young Turk of Real Estate Sector". He has won the prestigious CREDAI-MCHI Golden Pillar Award in the category of Best Debutant Real Estate Developer and has been awarded "Young Achiever of the Year" by ET NOW, CNN News 18, ZEE Business, MAHARASHTRA Times, ABP News, MID DAY and Realty Quarter.

Dr. Harshul has worked as EA to Ramesh Nair, CEO and Country Head at JLL, India and has worked in the Wealth Management Team at TATA Capital. He is a perfect blend of Corporate Experience along with stellar education credentials of Ph.D., LL.M, LL.B, MBA and BMS. Apart from this he is an NSE Certified Market Professional –

Level 4 and has done a course on 'Strategic Real Estate Management' from ISB, Hyderabad. As a matter of fact, he is one of the youngest Office Bearer in the Managing Committee of CREDAI-MCHI wherein he is the Convener of Research & Analytics Wing and looks into the Learning and Development Initiatives.

Dr. Harshul is also an Amazon Best Selling Author and has authored one of India's most comprehensive books on Real Estate Sector. Some of his books are: ERA Post RERA, Real Estate Laws, Reality of Realty, Real Estate Valuation, Affordable Housing, NBFC & HFC Crisis, Fractional Ownership & REITs, Insolvency & Bankruptcy Code, Self-Redevelopment & Reviving Stalled Projects, Luxury Retail and COVID-O-NOMICS. He regularly writes articles for fortnightly business magazine Property House.

Dr. Harshul is also a Visiting Faculty at the prestigious RICS School of Built Environment, Mumbai Campus. Harshul teaches the subject 'Real Estate Development Process' to Management Students at the Mumbai Campus. He is also Guest Lecturer at REMI – The Real Estate Management Institute, Mumbai. He was Invited to conduct Session on REITs in India for Developers Members of NAREDCO and was one of the youngest Member Developer to do so. He has also delivered a lecture at PEATA (I) on Future of Realty.

RESEARCH TEAM

Anushree Musale

PDGM – Real Estate Management (SBM NMIMS), B.E. Civil Engineering

Research Intern, M Realty

Archit Gadgil

BBA – Real Estate & Urban Infrastructure (RICS SBE)

Consultant, United Group of Builders and Developers

Harsh Dharasandiya

PDGM – Real Estate Management (SBM NMIMS), B.E. Civil Engineering

Research Intern, M Realty

Jeel Joshi

MBA – Real Estate and Urban Infrastructure (RICS SBE), Architect

Research Intern, M Realty

Mohd Shahid Tanwar

PDGM – Real Estate Management (SBM NMIMS), B.E. Civil Engineering

Intern, Kalpataru

Mohit Kamble

PDGM – Real Estate Management (SBM NMIMS), B.E. Civil Engineering

Research Intern, M Realty

Saurabh Pekhale

PDGM – Real Estate Management (SBM NMIMS), B.E. Civil Engineering

Research Intern, M Realty

Varun CH

PDGM – Real Estate Management (SBM NMIMS)

Research Intern, M Realty

Vishal Jain

MBA – Real Estate and Urban Infrastructure (RICS SBE)

Editor & Management Trainee, M Realty

CONTENTS

INTRODUCTION TO REAL ESTATE VALUATION

Have you ever wondered how a property is valued or what is the real worth of the house that you bought last summer? Should you care about it? Knowing the value of a property helps you to make affirmative decisions. Come along and dive into the world of valuation with us.

Valuation has been defined as the art or science of estimating values (Millington, 1982:4). It by and large means assessing the present worth of anything intangible or tangible.

Valuation dates back to the early days when the Barter system existed, back then the concept of money was not yet invented, and people use to exchange goods or services in return for other goods and services. Today valuing things is also a day-to-day activity in everyone's life, for example, if you want to buy a used cell phone, you estimate its price and evaluate whether it is overpriced or a steal deal. Likewise, valuing assets is also essential. Knowing the value/ worth of an asset is required for many critical decisions like choosing a property to invest in, deciding on the fair price to accept or pay while investing, or taking over an asset.

Valuation gives a reasonable estimate for all kinds of assets, be it real or financial assets. Over the past years, various methods have surfaced like the comparable method, residual method, income method, cost method, etc. The complexity of valuation varies from asset to asset and assignment to assignment, but the core principle remains the same. It is crucial to understand the basis of any valuation – a buyer would not be willing to pay more than an asset's worth.

This book describes various standards of valuations accepted and followed internationally. Further, it leans towards the valuation of immovable properties and understanding the different available valuation methods while focusing on specific asset classes like residential, commercial, hotel, and many more. The book concludes with a real-life case study and also describing other factors that affect valuation.

PURPOSE OF VALUATION

The purpose of property Valuation is determined by the client. Valuations performed by professionals can benefit in many ways; it provides a basis for decision-making regarding a real estate property. There are various reasons to assess the value of physical assets like real estate, and a valuation may be requested in several situations

2.1 Objective/Purpose of Valuation

a. **Purchase/Sale of property**

While buying or selling real estate or other physical assets, assessing the fair value becomes important to all the parties involved in the transaction. It helps avoid overvaluing or undervaluing the asset. In many cases, large public companies, trusts, or even individuals to protect their interests ask for professional help before selling or purchasing a property.

b. **Taxation**

Valuation of property is required under various direct tax laws administered by the Central Board of Direct Taxes, Ministry of Finance. These include the wealth tax act, capital gains tax, etc. Valuations are normally required to be done under a particular act for a specific purpose as of a specific date.

c. **Fixing Rent and Forecasting Earnings**

Any property owner would like to receive a return on his investment consistent with other investments' return. If the owner has constructed a building on his land to rent it or for any other purpose, he would like to work out the rent. From these rental incomes and expected outgoings, he can forecast the earning capacity of his property.

d. **Insurance**

Insurance policies can be made out against fire damage, theft, loss, and earthquake etc. Insured parties normally bring their valuation reports up-to-date at frequent intervals. If the property is over-insured, a higher premium is paid unnecessarily. On the other hand, if the property is underinsured, then actual losses cannot be recovered.

e. **Land Acquisition**

When a property is taken for a public project or public good, compensating the original owner at a fair market price is necessary. In such a case, the acquiring authority and the property owner may employ an independent valuer to determine the amount of compensation. The competent authority hears evidence from both sides and then decides on the compensation.

f. **Mortgages**

Property of various kinds can be pledged as a security against the loan. The property may be land, a residential house or any other asset. In such cases, a valuation report on the current market value of the property is necessary. The valuer should also give an idea of the property forecast, i.e. probable future trends regarding the property value. If the property is income-producing, the earning capacity of the property should be indicated. This data will allow the lender to set specific targets for repayment of loan and return of capital.

g. **Partition of Properties**

Distribution of property under a family settlement, will or on the dissolution of a partnership between various claimants, warrants valuation of the property. Such valuations form the basis of the settlement, or they may be used in any legal proceedings.

h. **Mergers and Acquisitions**

In case two or more businesses or enterprises come together, it is necessary to place a value on each so that stocks or shares of the newly merged corporation can be apportioned between shareholders. Also, when properties are exchanged, each asset should be valued.

i. **Liquidation**

It often happens that a company has become inefficient or is not operating for several reasons. There may be creditors of the company who appealed to the court for the liquidation process. In turn, the court may have appointed an 'official liquidator' to liquidate assets and pay off the creditors. The official liquidator will require an inventory of items and a minimum price at which the assets are sold. Here also valuation will be required for the liquidation proceedings.

j. **Leasing properties**

When properties are leased by an owner (lessor), it is necessary to determine the property's fair market value in monetary terms. Also, since the lessor is likely to ask for rent with the lease terms would first have to be settled. Valuation in such cases would include present value, estimated future life, annual maintenance costs, and rental value of the property.

k. **Accounting purpose**

Large companies have adopted a new concept of current cost accounting against traditional historical accounts to reflect a true picture of the balance sheet's prevailing fixed assets. Frequent valuation activities have to conducted to comply with this concept.

1. **Financial feasibility**

   Investors often need to choose between alternative investments options. Again, in each investment proposal, several questions are likely to arise, i.e., the cost of actual acquisition, the property's market value, the likely return on investment, etc.

The fair price of a building, factory, or land can be assessed through property valuation. Other reasons for valuation include Mesne profit, stamp duty recovery, auction bid, arbitration etc. Property valuation enables an individual or an organization to determine the property's worth and, defining the purpose of the valuation plays a key role.

ROLE AND COMPETENCIES OF A VALUER

The word competency is defined as the knowledge, skill, or ability to carry out a specific role or job. It helps in completing the task efficiently and effectively. A competency is split into specific tasks or skills. Every task or skill can be set out in specific behaviour at various levels of expertise. This chapter discusses the various skills and qualities that a professional valuer should possess.

3.1 Role of a Valuer/Professional Valuer

A valuer is a professional who carries out an examination to determine the market value of property or land. A professional valuer forms an opinion of value based on collected market evidence and his judgment backed by market analysis. A valuer plays a pivotal role in maintaining the smooth operations of the property market.

The job of a valuer can also be done by a real estate agent or qualified surveyor. A valuer's job is to prepare a report of a property with plans and photographs.

Buyers appoint valuers to perform property valuation if they are interested in buying property. Valuers also do council tax and rating levels to help local authorities. The other tasks involve credit facilities, acquisition, corporate management activities, securitization and feasibility studies, etc. A valuer is also bound by guidelines and practice directions issued by the board, such as Manual of Valuation Standards.

3.2 Competencies of a valuer

Professional knowledge and skills must be maintained to ensure that the client gets competent professional services built on present techniques, legislation and practices. A valuer should act tirelessly with relevant professional and technical standards.

A valuer should understand the economics of supply and demand in the real estate market, property law, meteorology, geography, building construction, statistical analysis, and accounting. All these learnings are driven from industry-based education, university education and the experience of valuation.

All the above skills can be encapsulated as,

- Practical experience
- Detailed market knowledge
- Technical expertise

Real estate property valuer can find the value of the different property types like commercial buildings, residential buildings, industrial buildings and business properties.

Other important skills of valuation are

- Vision
- Result-oriented
- Goal-oriented
- Performance optimization
- Team Player
- Long term oriented
- Analytical

Ethics is also an essential part that expands the capability of any valuer. It is categorized as the character, conduct, accountability and legal compliances. This can be achieved by the reputation a valuer holds.

Any individual should demonstrate a good character and reputation before being recognized as a professional valuer. A valuer should render a high standard of services, exercise independent professional judgement and due diligence and ensure proper care. A valuer shall clearly indicate to his customer, the services which he is qualified to provide and other services for which the client may have to appoint a different professional.

Overall qualities a property valuer should possess are-

- Character, skills and reputation
- Good analytical skills
- Good judgement
- Keep results confidential
- Provides wallet-friendly facilities
- Offers correct property assessment
- Prepare a detailed summary report

According to International Valuation Standard Council, the competency framework for Professional Valuers is categorized as-

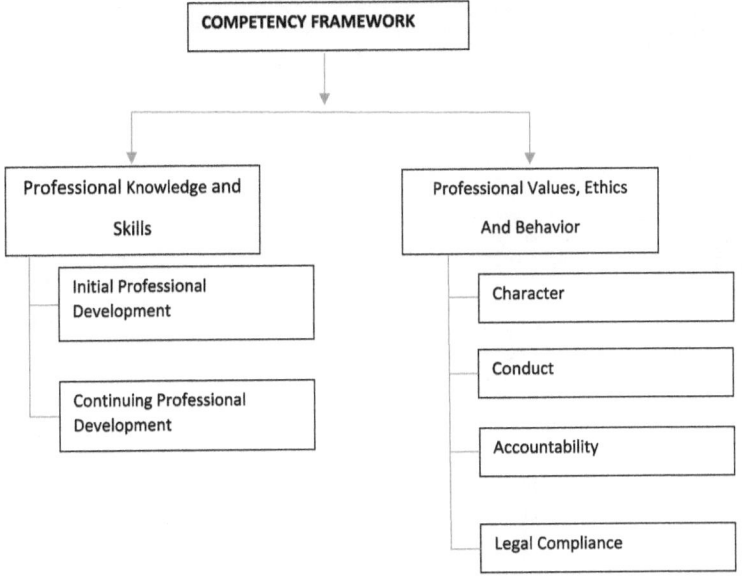

The competency framework ensures that valuers are competent to meet and practise the highest standards of professionalism required. The comprehensive skills and knowledge required by a professional valuer change with time due to the evolution of the disciplines and markets. Even though these competencies apply to all professional valuers, some may depend upon the valuer's seniority and role. The expectation of the valuer's performance generally increases when they progress through their careers.

STANDARDS OF VALUATION

Valuation is considered an inexact science which requires objectivity and subjectivity from the professional valuer. Thus, the skilled judgement offered by the valuers is vital in valuations. It is extremely critical to bring uniformity and consistency in this profession as a various set of assumptions taken by the valuers can bring drastic differences in values of assets.

Having uniform valuation standards lead to higher levels of transparency and comparability. In valuation, the practitioners and clients coordinate with various third-party organizations like financial institutions and banks. It is necessary to meet their expectations and establish a high level of credibility. This may be achieved by consistent and fair valuation practices by professionals. The international standardisation of valuation standards is required for benchmarking standards and performance, financial acceptability, reducing risk to the valuer and client while creating comparable standards worldwide. This leads to creating confidence and encouraging investment by various parties. Hence, all parties involved will be benefitted from knowing the international valuation standards and help the valuation professionals to operate in an accountable and transparent manner on a global level.

The profession of valuation is not regarded in the same terms as accountancy on a global level. A consistent approach to it in the form of international valuation standards will provide financial stability and instil trust in the marketplace. The goal of having uniform standards is for valuation professionals to jointly address the changes occurring in the world and offer high-quality services to the clients.

4.1 International Standards

International Valuation Standards Council (IVSC)

The International Valuation Standards Council (IVSC) is an independent organization that sets global standards for valuation. It is responsible for creating International Value Standards (IVS) that consist of information about the methods to conduct and report valuations, particularly those used by investors and other outside partners. The IVSC additionally promotes the need to build up a structure of direction on best practices for valuations of various assets and liabilities. It is recognized by the United Nations Department of Economic and Social Affairs and is headquartered in London, UK.

The core objectives of IVSC are:

a. Develop high-quality International Valuation Standards (IVS) that ensure consistency, transparency and confidence in valuations worldwide.

b. Encourage the adoption of IVS, along with valuation professionalism provided by Valuation Professional Organisations throughout the world.

The IVSC encourages coordinated effort and collaboration among its financial advisors, valuation and financial service providers, government controllers, global bodies, and academic bodies. The IVSC comprises more than 140 member organizations worldwide and numerous sponsors who are pioneers in the world of valuation.

The IVS comprises mandatory conditions that must be followed to express that the valuation was conducted in line with the IVS. The norms do not direct any specific strategy but give basic standards and principles that must be considered while performing a valuation.

The International Valuation Standards structure consists of the IVS framework, IVS General Standards and IVS Asset Standards.

Some of the member organizations which are exclusively related to real estate – Australian Property Institute, Real Estate Institute of Botswana, Finnish Association for Real Estate Valuation, Association of Professionals on Land and Realty, Israel Real Estate Appraisers Association, Japanese Association of Real Estate Appraisal, Korean Association of Property Appraisers, Lithuanian Association of Property Valuers, Ministry of Land Reform (Namibia), Property Institute of New Zealand, Institute of Philippine Real Estate Appraisers, Swiss Institute of Real Estate Appraisal and The Royal Institute of Charted Surveyors (RICS).

RICS Red book:

The RICS (Royal Institute of Charted Surveyors) is a professional body that promotes and enforces the highest international standards in the valuation, real estate, construction management and development of land and infrastructure. The 'Red Book' aims to provide an efficient framework within the rules of conduct so the user of valuation services can be confident of the end results.

RICS recognizes international Valuation Standards Council (IVSC) as the setter of international standards of valuation. RICS has for quite some time been a supporter of IVSC and has contributed significantly to the improvement of all specialized guidelines applying to a wide range of assets. RICS supports the continuous development and use of these standards by organizations and requires its members to follow these norms. The valuation principles and definitions of IVS are reflected in the *Red Book* as part of the framework and standards of RICS. The *Red Book* is compliant with the IVS principles. The *Red Book* wants to maintain greater accountability, transparency, comparability and availability of information globally in the profession of valuation.

The *Red Book* is divided into three parts: Professional standards (PS), Valuation Technical and Performance Standards (VPS) and Valuation Practice Guidance-Applications (VPGA). While PS and VPS are mandatory, VPGAs are mostly advisory and have further information to demonstrate good practice and a high professional competence level.

4.2 ICAI Recommended Standards

Amid the international valuation standards and the general RICS Red Book for valuation, been used as a reference in general, the Institute of Chartered Accountants of India (ICAI) recognised the need of having a uniform, consistent and transparent valuation practices across the nation. It constituted the Valuation Standards Board (VSB) with a fairly broad base of members and participants.

The VSB had an objective to identify sectors where valuation was needed and formulated such a set of valuation standards, which would be aligned with the globally accepted valuation practices. The aim and scope were to standardise the principles, practices and the procedures followed by valuers across industries and ensure uniformity and quality output.

The ICAI Valuation Standards are effective for the valuation reports issued on or after 1ˢᵗ July 2018 and are applicable for all valuation engagements on a mandatory basis under the Companies Act 2013. In respect of Valuation engagements under other statutes like Income Tax, SEBI, FEMA, etc., it is on a recommendatory basis for the Institute's members.

The ICAI includes eight valuations standards viz: 101, 102, 103, 201, 202, 301, 302, 303

1. ICAI Valuation Standard 101 – Definitions
2. ICAI Valuation Standard 102 – Valuation Bases

3. ICAI Valuation Standard 103 – Valuation Approaches and Methods

4. ICAI Valuation Standard 201 – Scope of Work, Analyses and Evaluation

5. ICAI Valuation Standard 202 – Reporting and Documentation

6. ICAI Valuation Standard 301 – Business Valuation

7. ICAI Valuation Standard 302 – Intangible Assets

8. ICAI Valuation Standard 303 – Financial Instruments

And also includes a framework for the preparation of valuation report following the ICAI valuation standards.

ICAI Valuation Standard 101 – Definitions

ICAI standard 101 prescribes certain definitions and principles which apply to the ICAI Valuation Standards, dealt specifically in other standards and form a basis for certain terms used in other standards.

(Reader should refer to ICAI Valuation Standard 101, Paragraph 6, for detailed definitions under the same.)

The terms defined in the stated Standard have a limited scope, i.e. it does not apply in valuation, where a valuer is required to use a definition prescribed by any law, regulations, rules or directions of any government or regulatory authority.

ICAI Valuation Standard 102 – Valuation Bases

The standard 102 defines the important valuation bases, i.e. fundamental principles on which the professional valuations are based, the assumptions on which a value is based and also explains the premises and scope of it.

Valuation base is the indication of the type of value being used in an engagement. Thus, the change of base, in turn, changes the conclusions of value.

Therefore, it is important to identify an appropriate base of valuation based on the purpose of valuation. ICAI Standard defines 3 valuation bases: (a) Fair value; (b) Participant specific value; and (c) Liquidation value.

Along with the valuation base, the premise of the value is also a significant consideration during valuation, i.e. the conditions and circumstances how an asset is deployed, wherein one or more premises may be adopted simultaneously. Some premises of value as per the ICAI are as follows: (a) highest and best use; (b) going concern value; (c) as is where is value; (d) orderly liquidation; or (e) forced transaction.

Other considerations during valuation may be participant-specific considerations depending on bases adopted or case to case basis and synergies, which indicates the combining effect on the value of two or more assets and liabilities. It is most significant in mergers and acquisitions and includes the details of integration costs and transaction costs.

ICAI Valuation Standard 103 – Valuation Approaches and Methods

The standard 103 defines the approaches and methods used for valuing an asset and guides the same. The standard does not apply in cases where a valuer is required to adopt valuation bases that are prescribed by a statute or regulation.

ICAI standard provides three main valuation approaches: (a) Market approach; (b) Income approach; and (c) Cost approach.

The market approach includes (a) Market Price method; (b) Comparable Companies Multiple Method; (c) Comparable Transaction Multiple Method and (d) Discount and control premium.

The income approach includes: (a) Discounted Cash Flow method; (b) Relief from Royalty (RFR) Method; (c) Multi-Period

Excess Earnings Method (MEEM); (d) With and Without Method (WWM) and (e) Option Pricing Models.

The cost approach includes: (a) Replacement Cost method and (b) Reproduction Cost Method; and elaborates further on the various methods, their subcategories and uses of each of them in specific areas.

The valuer may choose a basis of either a single valuation technique or a combination of multiple valuation techniques to perform the valuation.

ICAI Valuation Standard 202 – Reporting and Documentation

The standard 202 provides the standards regarding minimum requirements and a basis for preparing valuation report and appropriate documentation, which majorly depends on the nature of the engagement and the purpose of valuation as per the ICAI guidelines.

The valuer is supposed to do this in line with the valuation standards 102 and 103, which elaborates on the valuation basis and methods.

The reporting standard may also vary according to the type of asset valued and the client to which the valuer is catering to, in terms of written representations from the management, etc. The valuer needs to do the same keeping the Framework for valuation report in mind.

The standard also mentions the documentation requirements that the valuer needs to maintain, including the various records of valuation, evidence, procedures performed and the conclusions reached on a timely basis.

ICAI Valuation Standard 301 – Business Valuation

The standard 301 of ICAI Valuation Standard focuses on the valuation of businesses, ownership interest engagements, etc. to establish uniformity, providing a broad framework of generally accepted principles, theories and procedures.

The standard also mentions in brief about business valuation entities, valuation methodology, the premise of valuation and adjustment to information from financial statements, with due consideration of the treatment of non-operating assets, inter-company investments, the capital structure of the business, etc.

ICAI Valuation Standard 302 – Intangible Assets

The standard 302 gives specific guidelines and principles applicable for valuation of intangible assets as it forms a major requirement in financial reporting. The standard identifies an intangible asset as an identifiable non-monetary asset without physical substance like goodwill and also elaborates on various categories of intangible assets like (a) Customer-based intangible assets; (b) Marketing-based intangible assets; (c) Contract-based intangible assets; (d) Technology-based intangible assets and (e) Artistic-based intangible assets.

It also considers the purpose and objective of valuation, legal rights over intangible assets, evaluation of the highest best use considerations, laws and regulations guiding asset value in the country, economic useful life, discount rates and tax benefits of the same; along with elaborating ways and methodologies for valuation of intangible assets.

ICAI Valuation Standard 303 – Financial Instruments

The valuation standard 303 focuses on the valuation of financial instruments; establishes principles, and suggests methodologies and considerations.

As there are different usages and multiple categorisations of a financial instrument, the standard focuses on considering the purpose of valuation and features of the instrument being valued, in detail following the standards 102 and 103.

Along with details upon the various methods that can be used for valuation of financial instruments, the particular standard suggests the use of appropriate techniques in the circumstances for which sufficient data is available to measure the value. Thus, maximising the use of relevant observable inputs and accordingly minimising the use of unobservable inputs.

The standard further elaborates on the major considerations of, determining the present value, adjustments for credit risk and control environment for financial valuation.

4.3 Comparative Analysis

Comparison of ICAI Valuation Standards and IVS

ICAI	IVS
The objective of issuing the valuation standards is to standardize the various principles, practices and procedures followed by registered valuers and other valuation professionals for valuation of assets, liabilities, or a business.	The objective of the IVS is to increase the confidence and trust of users of valuation services by establishing transparent and consistent valuation practices.
Discount Rate is the return expected by a market participant from a particular investment. It shall reflect not only the time value of money but also the risk inherent in the asset being valued and the risk inherent in achieving the future cash flows.	Discount Rate is defined as the rate at which the forecast cash flow is discounted and should reflect the time value of money and the risks associated with the type of cash flow and the asset's future operations.

Continued...

The Comparable Transaction method involves valuing an asset based on transaction multiples derived from prices paid in transactions of assets to be valued.	The Comparable Transactions Method utilizes information on transactions involving assets similar to the subject asset to arrive at an indication of value.
The DCF Flow Method values the asset by discounting the cash flows expected to be generated by the asset for the explicit forecast period and the perpetuity value in case of assets with an indefinite life.	In the DCF Method, the forecasted cash flow is discounted back to the valuation date, resulting in the asset's present value. In some circumstances for long-lived assets, DCF may include a terminal value representing the asset's value at the end of the explicit projection period.
Income Approach is a valuation approach that converts maintainable or future amounts to a single current amount. The fair value measurement is determined based on the value indicated by current market expectations about those future amounts.	The income approach indicates value by converting future cash flow to a single current value. Under this approach, the value of an asset is determined by reference to the value of income, cash flow or cost savings generated by the asset
Market approach is a valuation approach that uses prices and other relevant information generated by market transactions involving identical or comparable assets, liabilities or a group of assets and liabilities, such as a business.	The market approach indicates value by comparing the asset with identical or comparable assets for which price information is available

In conclusion, these standards act as guidance and procedurals rules for professional valuers, thereby creating a framework for best practices and uniformity in the execution of valuations. They are simply procedural manuals and not valuation textbooks which define the methodology. However, there are several stand-alone papers and guidance notes that review and deal with various approaches to issues that arise in particular valuation cases.

VALUATION OF IMMOVABLE PROPERTIES

In principle, the value of a property is defined as the present value of all future benefits arising out of ownership. Benefits of a property are mostly realized over a long period, unlike several consumer goods. Hence, an assessment of the property's value should consider social, economic trends, environmental conditions, and governmental regulations that may impact the property's value.

However, to ascertain a fair value of individual properties, they should be subjected to appraisal with one of several methods. The valuation of immovable properties in real estate can be done by:

- Cost approach
- Income approach
- Market approach
- Belting and zoning methods

Each of them is further elaborated in detail.

5.1 Cost Approach

The cost approach is a method of valuing immovable property that calculates the price a buyer can pay for a piece of property is equal to the cost of constructing an equivalent. In the cost method, the property's value is proportional to land cost, plus total building costs, minus depreciation. Thus, there are two key market values to consider here: the building itself and the property on which it is located. The cost method values real estate properties based on how much the property will cost to repair it; or constructing an identical property. After factoring the property's value and deducting any decrease in the value of the house (depreciation of real estate), the cost method yields an exact market value.

Calculation

When it comes to valuing investment property with the cost approach, there are three main components. Land value, building expense, and depreciation of immovable property. The formula for approaching cost is

Market Value = Land Value + Building Construction Cost – Building Depreciation

Limitations Cost Approach

- Cost approach assumes that the buyer can find vacant land to build an identical property on it. If this assumption fails, the valuation of the property will be inaccurate.

- There may be difficulties in estimating the depreciation of older properties as there are many factors to be considered, which affects the valuation approach.

The two widely used methods under Cost Approach in Real estate are:

a. Contractors Method

b. Residual Method

5.1.1 Contractor's method

It is a valuation method used by contractors, investors, and even real estate developers to value unusual assets or assets that occasionally enter the market. This method is not highly recognized compared to the other valuation approaches. It is because the other property valuation approaches can be applied to most properties; and because property investors, developers, and valuation professionals are more familiar with them and know that they perform well.

This approach does have its drawbacks. The appraisal of two separate appraisers for the same property may have a significant difference. Therefore, this approach is used when no other evaluation method is available. If two evaluators are appointed for a property, and their values vary, then a medium value is selected as the final value.

The equation for the contractor's valuation method is:

Property Value = Cost of site + Construction Cost of Building

Limitations

- This method of appraisal is only applicable when there is no other method of appraisal is useful.

- When two different valuers are appointed for the same valuation assignment, there can be a huge difference between value opinion.

- When two different valuers are appointed for a property, and there is a difference in a value, the medium value is assumed as the final value.

- In a very comprehensive evaluation process of buildings, this method is used in combination with others method.

5.1.2 Residual method

The residual valuation method uses a very simple concept and calculation that helps developers determine a reasonable value for purchasing land or property. Typically, after doing so, the property developer can use it as a base cost to assess other spending components and the amount they can afford to spend on other fees such as site planning, land remediation, construction costs, professional fees and other fees in order to achieve a successful outcome of the project.

The approach does have its disadvantages, and knowledgeable practitioners should only use it. It is best achieved with a team of individuals who are experts in their particular process fields, be it real estate sales, growth, property maintenance or any other factor in the development project.

This approach is suitable when a person or company wishes to create or restore land, most often to be resold or used to profit in some other way. This is achieved on residential as well as commercial property. Before purchasing or building the property, this approach is also used to assess if the acquisition and construction would be successful after determining what is to be paid for the development land.

Developers must use this approach to avoid buying the land at a cost that will lose money rather than benefit from the project. A feasibility study should be performed to evaluate the optimal budget, thereby making the purchase and construction of the project viable. The residual method is a critical part of this study of growth and can include estimating several different costs that come with the production of the property. Any of these factors include (but certainly are not limited to) construction costs, construction time, return on investment, rent, finance costs, property taxes, fees, and any other added costs.

The equation for the residual valuation method is:

Land = Gross Development Value – (Construction + Fees + Profit)

Limitations

- Experienced valuers can only use this method of valuation.
- As the valuation is done at a single time point, this method is complicated because development takes time & method and focuses on the valuation of land development.

- The depth of valuation will depend on the role of valuation, the time required for the development process, and the asset type.

- The developer's profit element highly influence the final valuation.

5.2 Income Approach

According to ICAI, the income approach is the valuation method that converts maintainable or future amounts to a single current amount which can be discounted or capitalised.

It is primarily based on the evaluation of NPV of future cash flows based on fair value methods or intrinsic value methods. Income methods are used mostly when: (a) asset has no comparable product/transaction; (b) future cash flows can be projected reasonably, etc. Income approach can also be used in combination with other valuation methods, for example, in start-up companies, Real estate projects under development, etc.

The main types of valuation under the income approach are:

a. Discounted cash flow (DCF) method

b. Capitalization of earning method

While other methods under income approaches are: (a) Relief from Royalty method; (b) Multi-period excess earnings method; (c) With and without method; (d) Adjusted discounted cash flow method; (e) First Chicago method; (f) Options pricing models such as Black-Scholes or Binomial model, etc. All these other methods are a modification of the basic methods to suit different assets or businesses.

For example; First Chicago method uses the three scenarios of success, failure and survival case along with the basic method and associate's probabilities or weights to each case based on various factors such as market conditions, etc. At the same time, adjusted DCF method is used to judge the value of start-ups basis its potential to generate cash flow and adjusted with differential discount rates based upon risk perception.

MEEM, Relief from Royalty method, With and Without method are used only for valuation of intangible assets, and Option Pricing Models are used in case of valuation of options. Real Estate valuation by income approach is largely based on the discounted cash flow method and market capitalization method.

5.2.1 DCF method

ICAI defines the discounted cash flow method as to value the asset by discounting the cash flows expected to be generated by the asset for the explicit forecast period and the perpetuity value/terminal in case of assets with indefinite value. It is largely used for valuing businesses with definite cash flow, real estate projects and debt instruments.

The discounted cash flow (DCF) valuation method is of greatest application in assessing investment value to assist in buying/selling decisions or selecting available alternative investments. However, it can also be used to estimate Market Value by adopting a set of tenable assumptions consistent with observed market prices and applying those assumptions, with appropriate adjustments, to the valuation of the subject property. Where there are no transactions, the explicit DCF model provides a rational framework for the estimation of Market Value not present in the all-risks yield (capitalisation rate) approach, which relies on comparable to identify the all-risks yield.

The cash flow, discount rate and terminal value are the three essential inputs required in the DCF method. Analysing the future cash flows and assumptions for the same are crucial in predicting cash flows, i.e. whether pre-tax or post-tax cash flows are to be considered, or whether cash flow for equity or free cash flow to the firm is to be considered, etc. based on the asset being valued. Free Cash Flows to Firms (FCFF) and Free Cash Flow to Equity (FCFE) are the types of cash flows commonly used for projection of cash flows. Also, the forecast period is determined based on (a) Nature of asset; (b) Life of asset; (c) Sufficient period for an asset to reach a stable level of operating performance, etc.

To arrive at the estimated cash flows it is necessary to reflect the investment's specific leasing pattern including rent reviews, lease renewals or re-lettings on lease expiry, void costs while parts of the property are vacant, nonrecoverable outgoings and anticipated capital outlays on refurbishment or upgrade.

Cash flows should be prepared carefully to capture explicitly all information relating to income and expenditure. As and when appropriate, they should reflect rental growth, taxation, external financing, and all costs.

Discount rate, i.e. the second crucial input in DCF method, is the return expected from a particular market investment and reflects both time value of money and the risk inherent in achieving the particular discount rate and in achieving the future cash flows. The valuer needs to check the risks considered and see that the same risk factors need not be applied to the cash flows and discount rate both. The various types of discount rates used are: (a) cost of equity; (b) cost of debt; (c) weighted average cost of capital (WACC); (c) internal rate of return (IRR), etc., determination of which is more of a corporate finance aspect and is done by various methods such as (a) Capital Asset Pricing Model (CAPM) for the cost of equity; (b) Weighted Average Cost of Capital (WACC) is the combination of cost of equity and cost of debt weighted for their relative funding in the asset; (c) Build-up method which is generally used only in the absence of market inputs.

Lastly, a terminal value is a present value at the end of the explicit forecast period of all subsequent cash flows to the end of the asset's life. Terminal value is essential in case of assets having indefinite life or very long periods. The terminal value is usually determined by methods such as (a) Gordon (Constant) Growth model; (b) Variable Growth method; (c) exit multiple; (d) Salvage/Liquidation value

The exit valuation will reflect anticipated rental growth, the reversionary nature and unexpired terms of the leases at the exit date, and the application of an appropriate all-risks yield. Depending on the holding period, this may be forecast or based on equilibrium market conditions. The terminal growth rate used to calculate the terminal value, is evaluated by the valuer based on multiple factors such as (a) whether the level of operations beyond explicit forecast period is expected to be significantly different from the level projected in the last year of the explicit forecast period or only a normal growth is expected; (b) capacity utilisation at the end of explicit forecast period; (c) functional currency in which the projections have been prepared; (d) market share; (e) product life cycle; (f) geographic location of the asset; (g) type of cash flows; (h) residual life of the asset at the end of the explicit forecast period; (i) capital investment required to support the assumed growth rate; (j) whether there is a future growth potential for the asset beyond the explicit forecast period, or whether the asset is deteriorating in nature; and (k) for cyclical assets, the terminal value should consider the cyclical nature of the asset.

5.2.2 Valuation by Cap Rate method

The capitalization rate is the estimated percentage rate of return that an asset will produce on the owner's investment. In real estate, it refers to the rate of return on the property, based on the net operating income that the property generates and its market value.

$$\textit{Capitalization rate} = \frac{\textit{Net Operating Income}}{\textit{Current market value of asset}}$$

Where; Net Operating Income is the annual income generated by the property after deducting all expenses

Current market value is the value of an asset in the market place

It is mostly used to value multi-family properties and commercial properties more often by investors.

Lower cap rate shows lower net income, due to higher operating expenses, etc. (indicating lower profit from investment/lower revenue) and vice versa.

The cap rate is an indicator of risk as well, i.e. a lower cap rate indicates lower risk, and a higher cap rate indicates higher risk. Also, as capitalization rate goes up, the asset's valuation multiple goes down, as the rate also indicates the amount of time it takes to recover an investment in a property. For example, if a property has a cap rate as 10%, it will take 10 yrs. for an investor to recover his investment.

Thus, there is no optimum cap rate, and it depends on the investor's risk preference.

For the valuation of a particular property by cap rate method, the property's annual net operating income is evaluated and divided by the cap rate of similar properties in the vicinity to evaluate the market value. The same is again subject to multiple risk factors as cap rate does not change when markets are stable, but as the market condition changes cap rate changes along with it.

5.3 Market Approach

The market approach is a way of calculating the value of a given business, partnership interest, property or asset by utilizing techniques that compare it with identical organizations, partnership interests, or assets that were sold previously. The users should ensure that information used to value the given subject should be relevant and reliable.

Most people consult with real estate agents before listing their property as these agents have information about the prices for which similar properties in the neighbourhood were sold. They use the market approach method to estimate property value.

This method's main advantage is that the values used are the actual transaction prices and not estimated numbers based on assumptions. The data obtained can be verified and tested. Other methods require the valuers to develop assumptions to estimate future cash flows and other parameters. The basic format of this method is:

$$Value = (Price/Parameter)_{comp} \times Parameter_{subject}$$

There are two types of techniques used in the market approach method in valuation. They are:

a. Comparable transaction method

b. Guideline public company method

5.3.1 Comparable transaction method

In the comparable transaction method, the valuers use the transactional information of the assets comparable to the given asset to arrive at a value. In some contexts, the method is also referred to as prior transactions method or guideline transactions method.

If the information about the recent transactions is very limited, the prices of the similar properties listed for sale can also be considered. This is referred to as comparable listings method. While examining the listings, the commitment level also plays a role in assigning weight to the deals. The offer where the commitment to sell is high should be considered over offers with low commitment.

Different types of units can be used in the comparable transaction method, forming the foundation of the examination. In the case of business valuation, units like price/EBITDA multiples and price/revenue multiples are used whereas in real estate, units like price per square metre and rent per square metre area are used. For the valuation of financial instruments, units like return spreads and interest spreads are used. The units used may also vary according to geographical locations. Matrix pricing is a slightly different type of comparable transaction method used in valuing the financial instruments like debt securities. This method relies more on the relationship with other securities than on the quoted prices.

While comparing the given subject to the other comparable transactions, valuers may have to make adjustments according to physical dimensions, location of the asset, the asset's capability to make a profit, expected growth rate, marketability and any unusual terms.

The steps involved in performing valuation through this method are:

- Identifying the applicable units and suitable transactions which can be used for valuation
- Calculating the valuation metrics
- Conducting a qualitative and quantitative analysis between the assets and the given subject and modifying the metrics if necessary
- Finally, applying final valuation metrics to the given subject

5.3.2 Guideline public company method

In the guideline public method, a business's value is calculated based on trading metrics obtained from companies that are similar to the subject and are publicly traded. The subject company and the public company should be in the same industry. If no publicly traded companies are found in that industry, then companies similar in areas like markets served, growth and risks can be considered.

The differences between the comparable transaction method and guideline public method are that the trading multiples are readily available and that the public domain's information is as per standard accounting guidelines.

The steps involved in performing valuation through this method are:

- Identifying the comparable units and suitable public listed companies
- Conducting a qualitative and quantitative analysis between the public company and the given subject and modifying the metrics and risk factors if necessary
- Applying pricing multiples to the given subject

5.4 Belting Method

When a big size plot is to be valued, or a plot with less frontage and greater depth is to be valued, it is logical to adopt the belting method. It is due to the principle that the value of land in general decrease as the depth of the plot increases or in other words, the front land abutting road is more valuable than the rear land away from the road.

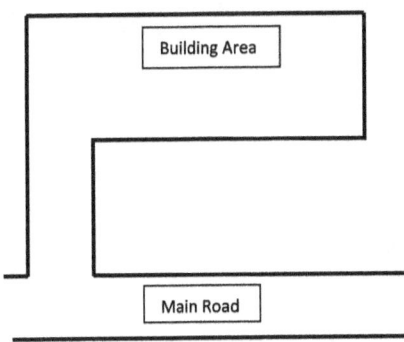

There are lands where the depth is much more than the width. Such types of lands are valued by the **belting method.**

While assessing the value of land, the depth plays a vital role. Front land has more value, which goes on decreasing as the depth increases. One has to assess which portion has the maximum value and from which portion its starts to reduce. The total extent is divided into many portions or belts, and different unit rates are adopted for each belt, and thus the total value is assessed. This is the simple principle of the belting method of valuation. In general, one may adopt the second belt's depth as 1.5 times the depth of the first belt. The depth of the third belt is 2.25 times the depth of the first belt (standard depth) is decided based on the reasonable price of property sold in the same area.

Rates of valuation:

- First belt = 100% of the prevailing rate (D)
- Second belt = 67% of the prevailing rate (1.5 D)
- Third belt = 50% of the prevailing rate (2.25 D)

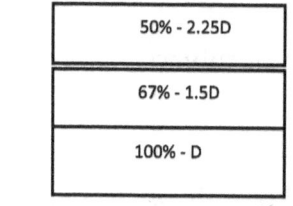

The Criteria of belting systems: Valuation by the belting method can be done if the land is vast. It is not possible to subdivide the plot legally. Comparable sale instances for similar lands are not available.

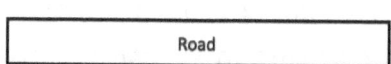

- If the depth is more.
- The vast land has road only on one boundary.

This method is not suitable for:

- If it is a small plot.
- If it has two roads (or corner plots)
- If it is an agricultural land
- If F.S.I controls the development.

5.5 Zoning Method

The zoning method was invented in the 1950s and is used to compare rents of retail or shops of different layout or sizes. It is used by both the private and public sector surveyors. According to this method, the retail space is divided into zones named A, B, C, etc. Zone A gets more rent compared to the other zones. The shop's front will fetch more rent than the back, as the front is easily visible to the pedestrians. The ground floor is only included in zoning if there is a first floor or a storeroom after the building's structural wall, it is rated, but it is not a part of the zoned area. Zoning takes into account the different sizes and shapes of the shop when looking in the rental value. This method uses ITZA, which means "in terms of zone A". You'll need a net area survey (schedule area) of the space and a sketched plan to use this method.

Zones are divided as follows:

- Each zone covers the width of the building and extends back 6.1m.

- Zone A is the first 6.1m, Zone B the next 6.1m, zone C the next 6.1m, and remaining is called the remainder zone. A zone can further be divided into four zones. Refer to fig 1.

- Area of the zone should be a net area which means the area of the stair, stairwells, columns, wc, etc. should be subtracted from the internal area of the zone

- Value of zone B is half the value of zone A; the value of zone C is half the value of zone B, and so on.

- Zoning is only applied to the ground floor areas only

- The of zoning stops at the first structural wall running across the width of the building.

Zone	Value ITZA (in terms of zone A)	Zone D*
A	A	
B	A/2	
C	B/2	
D (Reminder zone)	C/2	

* reference from http://www.beckettkay.co.uk/a-note-on-zoning/ &   D* is reminder zone
https://www.youtube.com/watch?v=KEExbXFv-JM   Figure no:- 1

In figure one, zone A is the entrance of the retail or shop. And the whole area is divided by 6.1 m equally till zone c and the rest area is demarked as a remainder zone.

Zoning is not always used for all shop or retail spaces; departmental stores and big supermarkets are valued on overall price per square meter basis as the front of this shop is not that important for sales.

In addition to the heads discussed above, other methods are also used frequently. For example, few industry professionals have an active working knowledge of the city's development and migration patterns, with which they determine the localities that will probably experience the highest rate of appreciation. Irrespective of the approach being used, the success of the same is dependent on how thoroughly it has been researched.

The bottom line is that true property valuation is important to buyers and sellers, mortgage lenders, insurers investors of real property and even though professionals and experts mostly perform valuations, anyone involved in property transactions could benefit from acquiring a fundamental understanding of the various methods of real estate valuation.

VALUATION OF VARIOUS
ASSET CLASSES

Valuation of real property is determined by subjecting it to a particular valuation method or a combination of such methods. The approach is adopted depending on the nature of the asset class and the extent of information available. For example, the valuation of a single-family home may be conducted using the market approach. In contrast, a commercial property with no comparable sale transactions may be valued using cost or income approach. A valuer needs to study the asset class in detail and collect all information before conducting the valuation. This chapter reviews (with illustration) the various real estate asset classes with suitable valuation approaches that need to be adopted.

6.1 Residential

There are two ways of valuing a Residential Project. Residential Valuation model differs from developer to developer. It differs based on how the developer has opted to raise finance for his/her project. The timelines committed by the developer also has a significant impact on the Valuation of a project.

The First way of Valuation is a Direct Comparison. It is the easiest method of valuation. Comparable projects are identified, the sale rate is given discount/premium based on the advantage the said project has over the other.

Attributes	Subject Property	Instance 1	D/P (%)	Instance 2	D/P (%)
Location	Plot 52, Sector 47	Sector 47, Dronagiri New, Mumbai, Maharashtra	0.00%	Sector 51, Dronagiri New, Mumbai, Maharashtra	5.00%
Accessibility	Internal Panvel-Uran Road	Internal Panvel-Uran Road	0.00%	Internal Panvel-Uran Road	0.00%
Neighbourhood Profile	Predominantly residential developments	Predominantly residential developments	0.00%	Predominantly residential developments	0.00%
Type of instance		Quoted	-5.00%	Quoted	-5.00%
Total Premiums/Discounts			-5.00%		0.00%
Sale Rate of Individual Flat (Carpet)		15,000		15,500.00	
Achievable Sale Rate of Individual Flat (Carpet)		14,250.00		15,500.00	
Weighted Average		50.00%		50.00%	
Achievable Rate of Subject Property	14875.00				

In this example, consider individual flats of two different comparable building in Dronagiri. By employing the above method, we can calculate the individual flat's sale rate and multiple it by the total number of flats in the subject property. By deducting costs that we will incur, the residential project can be valued.

The other method of Valuating a residential Project is DCF analysis. This method takes into accounting Time Value of Money, project timelines and Sales Schedule for a project.

Area Statement			
Sr No.	Particulars	Area (sqm)	Area (sq. ft)
1	Land Area	10,000	1,07,620
2	Less: RG	1,500.00	16,143
3	Net Plot area for construction	8,500	91,477
4	Base FSI	1.33	–
5	Base FSI Area	11,305	1,21,664
6	Premium FSI	0.84	–
7	Premium FSI Area	7,140.00	76,841
8	TDR	0.83	–
9	TDR Area	7,055.00	75,926
10	Built Up Area	25,500	2,74,431
11	Fungible Area @35%	8,925	96,051
12	Gross Built Up Area	34,425	3,70,482
13	Gross Carpet Area	27,540	2,96,385

Cost Statement			
Sr No.	Particulars	Cost INR Per Sq. ft	Comments
1	Land Cost		
	Approval Costs	350	On Built Up
	Site Development Cost	60	On Built Up
2	Construction cost	3,100	On built Up
	Escalation of Cost of Construction	5%	Year On Year
3	Professional Fees	3%	applied over
4	Admin Expenses	3%	applied over
5	Contingency	5%	applied over
6	Marketing Expense	4%	applied over

Revenue Statement			
Sr No.	Particulars	INR on Carpet Area	Area in Sq. ft
1	Sales	32,000	
2	Escalation on sales Price	3%	

Phasing of Development

Sr No.	Particulars	FY '19-'20	FY '20-'21	FY '21-'22	FY '22-'23	FY '23-'24	Total
1	Construction of BUA over Years	20%	30%	15%	20%	15%	100%
	Total BUA Constructed in Sq. ft in INR	74,096	1,11,145	55,572	74,096	55,572	3,70,482
2	Cost of Construction per Sq. ft in INR	3,100.00	3255	3418	3589	3768	
3	Total Cost of Cost of Construction	230	362	190	266	209	1,257
4	Approval cost Phasing	40%	10%	10%	10%	30%	100%
	Approval cost	52	13	13	13	39	130
5	Site Development Cost in INR	5,10,000	0	0	0	0	5,10,000
6	Professional Fees	34	0	0	0	0	34
7	Admin Expenses	34	0	0	0	0	34
8	Contingency Expense	57	0	0	0	0	57
9	Sales Over the Years	20%	15%	15%	20%	30%	100%
	Sales Price Escalation In INR per Sq. ft	32,000	32,800	33,620	34,461	35,322	
	Total Sales	1,897	1,458	1,495	2,043	3,141	10,033
10	Marketing Expense Break up	30%	10%	10%	20%	30%	100%
	Marketing Expense	120	40	40	80	120	401

Sr No.		FY '19-'20	FY '20-'21	FY '21-'22	FY '22-'23	FY '23-'24
	NPV Calculation					
	Outflows					
1	Total Cost of Cost of Construction	528	402	230	359	369
2	Approval cost	72	18	18	18	54
3	Site Development Cost	6	0	0	0	0
4	Professional Fees	40	0	0	0	0
5	Admin Expenses	40	0	0	0	0
6	Contingency Expense	67	0	0	0	0
7	Marketing Expense	102	34	34	68	102
	Total Inflows	856	454	282	445	524
1	Total Sales	2,159	1,652	1,685	2,291	3,506
2	EBITDA	1,303	1,198	1,403	1,846	2,981
	NPV Calculation					
1	18% discounting year on Year	0.85	0.72	0.61	0.52	0.44
2	Net Flow	1,104	860	854	952	1,303
3	Developers Profit (25%)	2,508				
4	NPV	2,565				
5	Realizable Value (reduction of 10%)	2,309				

Consider the Example of a Residential Tower in Wadala. The Plot Area is assumed to be 10,000 sqm. and F.S.I calculation are as per the DPCR of Mumbai. The Cost and Sales rate are assumptions and are subject to change from developer to developer.

This example demonstrates how a phasing of a project is done. The calculated NPV considers the Time value of Money Concept and provides a more realistic residential project value. This is the way residential projects are valued.

6.2 Commercial

Valuation of a commercial property plays a vital role in determining the asset's performance as part of a portfolio. Most appraisers opt for 'Sales Comparison Approach' with residential properties, but commercial Real Estate valuation is a different ballgame altogether. The challenge with using this method is finding a comparable property for commercial real estate could be difficult. Sometimes, the appraiser may have to look well outside the micro-market, making unreliable comparisons and inaccurate valuation.

In the cost approach, it is assumed that the commercial property's value is equivalent to the cost incurred to re-construct it in current time. The method fails to capture the income-generating potential of the property. It is most useful when the property is located in a comparatively inactive area where the data availability for the alternate approaches is hard to come by. It can also be used for the under-construction property or the ones that are fully constructed but not in a working state currently.

In the following example, commercial property is assumed to be located in a remote area and is not in a working state. The appraiser uses the cost approach to arrive at the market value of the property:

PARTICULARS	
Cost of land per sq. ft.	₹ 8,075
Plot area	392040 sq. ft.
Total cost of land	**₹ 3,16,57,23,000**
Cost of construction per sq. ft.	₹ 3,125
Total leasable area	400000 sq. ft.
Total BUA	571430 sq. ft.
Cost of construction (superstructure)	₹ 1,78,57,18,750
Cost of basement construction per sq. ft.	₹ 2,250
Total area of basement	74000 sq. ft.
Cost of construction (basement)	₹ 16,65,00,000
Total cost of construction	**₹ 1,95,22,18,750**
Life of building	60
Depreciation per year (Cost of construction/Life of building)	₹ 3,25,36,979.17
Age of the building	10 years
Total depreciation	**₹ 32,53,69,791.67**
FORMULA	
Total cost of land + Total cost of construction – Depreciation	**₹ 4,79,25,71,958**

Table 1 Valuation of the commercial building by cost approach method

The income approach is the most suitable approach for a commercial property that is fully constructed and in operating condition. Since the DCF method of income approach is based on how the subject property is expected to generate income in the future, It captures the asset's income-generating capacity.

Many commercial properties have lease payments as their major source of income. The net operating income (NOI) from expected income and estimated expenses is forecasted. This NOI is discounted into the current value to determine the present value. The discount rate used for the DCF method is directly comparable to the risk associated with valuation assumptions. Highly volatile income projections will require a high discounting rate.

The same subject property as above is considered for the valuation of a commercial property by the DCF method of the income approach. The following are the assumptions required for it:

PARTICULARS	
Period considered for cashflows	2021-2030
Lease period for tenant	9 Years
REVENUE ASSUMPTIONS	
Occupancy rate (tenants)	91%
Average rent per sq. ft./month (present)	₹ 141
Food Court occupancy	95%
Food Court rentals per sq. ft./month	₹ 65
Rent Escalation (every 3 years)	6%
EXPENSES ASSUMPTIONS	
Property tax per sq. ft./month	₹ 3.50
Escalation in property tax (every 5 years)	40%
Discount rate	17%
Corporate Tax rate	25.17%
Caprate for terminal value	8.50%

The tenants' occupancy rate is calculated by analysing the current lease agreements of the existing tenants and their balance lease years. Analysis of lease agreements and micro-market research will help the appraiser conduct a more accurate commercial property valuation.

Weighted Average Cost of Capital (WACC) is considered the discount rate for the subject property's cashflows. The calculations of WACC were based on the general current rates in the market. The formula for WACC is as given below:

WACC = (Cost of Debt x Weightage of Debt)
+ (Cost of Equity x Weightage of Equity)

PARTICULARS	
Interest rate for LAP (cost of debt)	8.75%
Debt ratio (Weight of debt)	50%
Average return on private equity investment (cost of equity)	25%
Equity ratio (Weight of Equity)	50%
WACC (discount rate)	**17%**

The above assumptions are used to conduct the valuation of the subject property by the Discounted cash flow (DCF) method of the income approach. The cashflow projections of 10 years are used to achieve the NOI of each year. The NOI is discounted at a suitable discount rate. The property's terminal value for the 10th year is calculated by the income capitalization approach at a suitable caprate. The calculated terminal value is added to the NOI of the 10th year. The net present value is the fair market value of the property. The formula for the terminal value of the property:

$$\text{Terminal value} = \frac{\text{(NOI of 10}^{th}\text{ year)}}{\text{Caprate}}$$

PARTICULARS		YEAR 2021	YEAR 2022	YEAR 2023	YEAR 2024	YEAR 2025	YEAR 2026	YEAR 2027	YEAR 2028	YEAR 2029	YEAR 2030
Total number of leasing months		12	12	12	12	12	12	12	12	12	12
Total Leasable area (sq. Ft)		4,00,000	4,00,000	4,00,000	4,00,000	4,00,000	4,00,000	4,00,000	4,00,000	4,00,000	4,00,000
Occupancy rate		91%	94%	94%	94%	94%	94%	94%	95%	95%	95%
Total leasable area in a year (sq. ft)		4358400	4512000	4512000	4512000	4512000	4512000	4512000	4560000	4560000	4560000
Average rent per sq ft / month	6%	₹141	₹149	₹149	₹149	₹158	₹158	₹158	₹167	₹167	₹167
Annual Revenue from leasing		₹61,27,91,040	₹67,24,50,432	₹67,24,50,432	₹67,24,50,432	₹71,27,97,458	₹71,27,97,458	₹71,27,97,458	₹76,36,03,234	₹76,36,03,234	₹76,36,03,234
Revenue from food court	95% Occupancy	₹91	₹96	₹96	₹96	₹102	₹102	₹102	₹108	₹108	₹108
	3,70000 sq.Ft	₹38,38,38,000	₹40,68,68,280	₹40,68,68,280	₹40,68,68,280	₹43,12,80,377	₹43,12,80,377	₹43,12,80,377	₹45,71,57,199	₹45,71,57,199	₹45,71,57,199
Annual Interest on security deposit (7% on rent of 6 months)	7%	₹23,36,93,991	₹24,21,66,866	₹24,21,66,866	₹24,21,66,866	₹24,21,66,866	₹24,21,66,866	₹24,21,66,866	₹30,46,77,690	₹30,46,77,690	₹30,46,77,690
TOTAL ANNUAL REVENUE		₹1,23,03,23,031	₹1,32,14,85,578	₹1,32,14,85,578	₹1,32,14,85,578	₹1,38,62,44,701	₹1,38,62,44,701	₹1,38,62,44,701	₹1,52,54,38,124	₹1,52,54,38,124	₹1,52,54,38,124
EXPENSES											
Building repairs per sq. ft / month	4%	₹18.0	₹18.7	₹19.5	₹20.2	₹21.1	₹21.9	₹22.8	₹23.7	₹24.6	₹25.6
Annual building repair expenses		₹8,64,00,000.0	₹8,98,56,000.0	₹9,34,50,240.0	₹9,71,88,249.6	₹10,10,75,779.6	₹10,51,18,810.8	₹10,93,23,563.2	₹11,36,96,505.7	₹11,82,44,365.0	₹12,29,74,140.6
Property tax per sq. Ft	₹3.50	₹3.5	₹3.5	₹3.5	₹3.5	₹3.5	₹4.9	₹4.9	₹4.9	₹4.9	₹4.9
Total Property tax		₹1,68,00,000	₹1,68,00,000	₹1,68,00,000	₹1,68,00,000	₹1,68,00,000	₹2,35,20,000	₹2,35,20,000	₹2,35,20,000	₹2,35,20,000	₹2,35,20,000
Total Annual Expenses		₹10,32,00,000	₹10,66,56,000	₹11,02,50,240	₹11,39,88,250	₹11,78,75,780	₹12,86,38,811	₹13,28,43,563	₹13,72,16,506	₹14,17,64,366	₹14,64,94,141
Net Annual income		₹1,12,71,23,031	₹1,21,48,29,578	₹1,21,12,35,338	₹1,20,74,97,329	₹1,26,83,68,922	₹1,25,76,05,890	₹1,25,34,01,138	₹1,38,82,21,618	₹1,38,36,73,758	₹1,37,89,43,983
PAT	25.17%	₹84,34,26,164.11	₹90,90,56,973.56	₹90,63,67,403.77	₹90,35,70,253.18	₹94,91,20,464.03	₹94,10,66,487.79	₹93,79,20,071.55	₹1,03,88,06,236.97	₹1,03,54,03,073.16	₹1,03,18,63,782.80
Terminal value	8.90%										₹12,13,95,73,915
Net Annual cashflows		₹84,34,26,164	₹90,90,56,974	₹90,63,67,404	₹90,35,70,251	₹94,91,20,464	₹94,10,66,488	₹93,79,20,072	₹1,03,88,06,237	₹1,03,54,03,073	₹13,17,14,37,698
Fair market price of the property	17% Discount rate	₹8,83,33,40,140									

55

6.3 Hotel

Hotel is categorized as a Trade Related Property (TRP). A TRP is a property that consists of buildings or structures built to cater to a specific type of business activity. Since the building's use is limited to a particular activity, the property's value is usually inherently linked with its trading potential in that location (unless a substitute purpose holds more value). A hotel property typically can be used as just a hotel without any drastic altercations. Hence, the property's value will be closely related to the profitability potential of the hotel business operating in that property. Based on the mentioned criteria, the income capitalization approach is the most relevant method for valuing hotel assets.

In the income approach, the Discounted Cashflow (DCF) method is implemented to estimate the property's current open market value. This approach is apt for the valuation of dynamic hotels as it considers the expected benefits that the hotel property can be delivered in the future years. Traditionally, investors prefer a cash flow projection of at least ten years to estimate its value. The projected net cash flows are discounted at a suitable rate with respect to the various market conditions to find the present value. The hotel property's terminal value is added to the final year cashflows to conclude the property's final open market value. The negative cashflows like land cost and construction cost are not considered for an existing property.

Based on the assumptions, the subject hotel property's cash flows are projected for the next ten years to estimate the property's market value. The calculated Net Present Value of all the cash flows (including the terminal value) is the hotel property's estimated market value.

Thus, the market value of the subject hotel property is ₹ 32,95,27,618.02 (₹32.95 Crore).

PARTICULARS	YEAR 1	YEAR 2	YEAR 3	YEAR 4	YEAR 5	YEAR 6	YEAR 7	YEAR 8	YEAR 9	YEAR 10
No. of nights	365	365	365	365	365	365	365	365	365	365
No. of rooms	108	108	108	108	108	108	108	108	108	108
Occupancy rate	60%	60%	65%	65%	70%	70%	75%	75%	80%	80%
Room nights sold in a year	23652	23652	25623	25623	27594	27594	29565	29565	31536	31536
ARR	₹7,200	₹7,452	₹7,713	₹7,983	₹8,262	₹8,551	₹8,851	₹9,160	₹9,481	₹9,813
Annual room revenue	₹17,02,94,400	₹17,62,54,704	₹19,76,25,587	₹20,45,42,482	₹22,79,86,198	₹23,59,65,715	₹26,16,69,123	₹27,08,27,542	₹29,89,93,606	₹30,94,58,383
F&B, conference room, Ball room revenue	₹50,00,000	₹51,75,000	₹53,56,125	₹55,43,589	₹57,37,615	₹59,38,432	₹61,46,277	₹63,61,396	₹65,84,045	₹68,14,487
Total Annual Revenue	₹17,52,94,400	₹18,14,29,704	₹20,29,81,712	₹21,00,86,072	₹23,37,23,813	₹24,19,04,146	₹26,78,15,399	₹27,71,88,938	₹30,55,77,652	₹31,62,72,869
EXPENSES										
Departmental Expenses										
F&B, Conference room & ball room	₹15,00,000.0	₹15,52,500.0	₹16,06,837.5	₹16,63,076.8	₹17,21,284.5	₹17,81,529.5	₹18,43,883.0	₹19,08,418.9	₹19,75,213.6	₹20,44,346.0
Other expenses	₹6,81,17,760.0	₹7,05,01,881.6	₹7,90,50,234.7	₹8,18,16,993.0	₹9,11,94,479.1	₹9,43,86,285.8	₹10,46,67,649.1	₹10,83,31,016.8	₹11,95,97,442.6	₹12,37,83,353.1
Operating expenses										
Maintenance cost	₹1,70,29,440.0	₹1,76,25,470.4	₹1,97,62,558.7	₹2,04,54,248.2	₹2,27,98,619.8	₹2,35,96,571.5	₹2,61,66,912.3	₹2,70,82,754.2	₹2,98,99,360.6	₹3,09,45,838.3
Marketing	₹17,02,944.0	₹17,62,547.0	₹19,76,255.9	₹20,45,424.8	₹22,79,862.0	₹23,59,657.1	₹26,16,691.2	₹27,08,275.4	₹29,89,936.1	₹30,94,583.8
Administration	₹17,02,944.0	₹17,62,547.0	₹19,76,255.9	₹20,45,424.8	₹22,79,862.0	₹23,59,657.1	₹26,16,691.2	₹27,08,275.4	₹29,89,936.1	₹30,94,583.8
License fees	₹42,57,360.0	₹44,06,367.6	₹49,40,639.7	₹51,13,562.1	₹56,99,654.9	₹58,99,142.9	₹65,41,728.1	₹67,70,688.6	₹74,74,840.2	₹77,36,459.6
Energy	₹1,19,20,608	₹1,23,37,829	₹1,38,33,791	₹1,43,17,974	₹1,59,59,034	₹1,65,17,600	₹1,83,16,839	₹1,89,57,928	₹2,09,29,552	₹2,16,62,087
Fixed expenses										
Property tax	₹35,05,888	₹36,28,594	₹40,59,634	₹42,01,721	₹46,74,476	₹48,38,083	₹53,56,308	₹55,43,779	₹61,11,553	₹63,25,457
Insurance	₹17,52,944	₹18,14,297	₹20,29,817	₹21,00,861	₹23,37,238	₹24,19,041	₹26,78,154	₹27,71,889	₹30,55,777	₹31,62,729
Management Fees	₹61,35,304	₹63,50,040	₹71,04,360	₹73,53,013	₹81,80,333	₹84,66,645	₹93,73,539	₹97,01,613	₹1,06,95,218	₹1,10,69,550
Total Annual Expenses	₹11,76,25,192	₹12,17,42,074	₹13,63,40,385	₹14,11,12,298	₹15,71,24,844	₹16,26,24,213	₹18,01,78,394	₹18,64,84,638	₹20,57,18,829	₹21,29,18,988
Net Annual Cashflow	₹5,76,69,208	₹5,96,87,630	₹6,66,41,327	₹6,89,73,774	₹7,65,98,969	₹7,92,79,933	₹8,76,37,005	₹9,07,04,300	₹9,98,58,823	₹10,33,53,882
PAT (25% tax applicable)	₹4,32,51,906.00	₹4,47,65,722.71	₹4,99,80,995.38	₹5,17,30,330.22	₹5,74,49,226.59	₹5,94,59,949.52	₹6,57,27,753.72	₹6,80,28,225.10	₹7,48,94,117.08	₹7,75,15,411.17
Present value (IRR 20%)	₹3,60,43,255.0	₹3,10,87,307.44	₹2,89,24,187.14	₹2,49,47,111.41	₹2,30,87,555.70	₹1,99,13,016.79	₹1,83,43,409.78	₹1,58,21,190.93	₹1,45,14,981.64	₹1,25,19,171.66
Terminal Value (at caprate of 12%)										₹10,43,26,430.54
Net present Value of the property										₹32,95,27,618.02

57

6.4 Retail and Warehousing

Valuing a Retail property:

Valuation of Retail Property is fundamentally different compared to the valuation of other Real Estate Asset Class. Value of retail space is directly related to the amount of business a said property can deliver. If we consider this as the focal point, we can understand the difference between a Retail Property and a Commercial Property. A Commercial Property is not valued upon the business a tenant is making in a year. Consider the Amazon Office in BKC, the company brings in millions of dollars of revenue in India but only pays about 300 Rs. per sq. ft.

Valuation of Retail Space done based on Cost Approach would also be inaccurate. It would completely discount the business environment, the people's spending capacity in the neighbourhood, Customer buying behaviour, etc. Let's take an example of a shop in Connaught Place, Delhi. A typical 150 sq. ft. (Carpet) shop can be built at the rate of 2500 Rs. per sq. ft. Land rate of the same area is approximately 5000 per sq. ft. This means the Shop would cost us a total of 11.25 lakh Rupees. However, the current price for the same space could go up to 2 Cr.

Therefore, the valuation of the retail property must be done employing certain methods to get accuracy.

There are two methods by which a retail space can be valued accurately.

1. Direct Comparison: This method considers the transactional history of the area, land rate, buying patterns, possible business income, Spending Capacity, etc. Comparable properties in terms of nature of Business, size, frontage, etc. can be used to compare the subject property. Comparable properties need not be similar, and certain changes can be made to derive a

value appropriate to our subject property. The instances used can be actual Transaction or quoted transaction.

For Example: Consider our Subject Property to be a shop of 500 sq. ft. in FIFC, BKC. The Valuation of the retail property is shown below.

Attribute	Subject Property	Comparable 1	D/P	Comparable 2	D/P
Name of the property	First International Financial Center	First International Financial Center		One BKC	
Location	Internal Bandra-Kurla Complex Road, Mumbai	Internal B K C Road, BKC, Mumbai	0.00%	Internal B K C Road, BKC, Mumbai	0.00%
Area (sq. ft.)	500	900	-5.00%	600	0.00%
Connectivity, Visibility & Frontage	Connected through internal BKC Road (off BKC Link Road); Visible from internal BKC Road	Connected through internal BKC Road (off BKC Link Road); Visible from internal BKC Road		Connected through internal BKC Road (off BKC Link Road); Visible from internal BKC Road	
Type of Instance		Transacted Instance	0.00%	Transacted Instance	0.00%
Year of Transaction		2018, Q3	2.50%	2018, Q4	2.50%
Total Adjustment			-2.50%		2.50%
Benchmark Rental Rate on Leasable (INR / sq ft)		40,000.00		42,000.00	
Achievable Rental Rate (INR / sq ft)		39,000.00		43,050.00	
Weightages of Comparable		50%		50%	
Achievable Rental Rate on Leasable Area (INR / sq ft)					27,350
Achievable Rental Rate on Leasable Area (INR / sq ft) Rounded Off					27,350
Achievable Market Value					1,36,75,000
Estimated Value (INR) Rounded Off					1,36,75,000

Here we have taken two comparable properties. Comparable 1 is in the same building, although the size is larger. We need to discount the rate of property to make it similar to our subject property. The same is done with Comparable 2. The Comparable 1 was transacted in the year 2018, and the rate has gone up since then. Therefore we have given a certain premium for the same. The rate of Premium and Discount can be given by market understanding.

In this manner, a Retail Property can be valued using historical transactions and comparable properties in the neighbourhood.

There is a certain backdrop of using Direct Comparison Method to Value the Retail Properties. The spaces which are unique and don't have comparable cannot be accurately valued; it would be like comparing Apples with Oranges. Thankfully the other method to value retail property tackles this problem.

2. Valuation by Income Approach: This method considers the income of a said business and values the property accordingly. The income can be a future estimate or actual income of the business depending upon the case.

Value of the Property = (Net operating Income)/(Cap Rate)

INFLOW	INR
Total Leaseable Area in sq.ft.	10,000
Monthly Rent	13,00,000.00
Monthly weighted average rent on carpet /sq.ft. (excluding property tax and CAM charges)	130
Total annual base rent	1,56,00,000
TOTAL INFLOW	1,56,00,000
OUTFLOWS	INR
CAM	7,20,000
TOTAL OUTFLOWS	7,20,000
Capital Value Assesment	INR
Net Cash Flow	1,48,80,000.00
Cap/ Yield Rate	8.0%
Total Capitalization Value	18,60,00,000.00
Total Capitalization Value per sq.ft.	18,600.00

Valuation by such method is derived from the above formula. The Net Operating Income is income that a said property can generate minus expenses such as Common Area Maintenance (CAM) and Property Tax.

For example, let's Consider a Rental Property in Andheri, 10,000 sq. ft. in size rented out for a rate of 130 per sq. ft. The CAM Charges for the said property are 6 Rs. per sq. ft. per month.

> Following the above methods of adding up inflows and subtracting outflows will derive the Net Operating Income. By using the above formula Value of the Asset can be derived.

> Note Capitalization rate or the Cap rate is arbitrary and depends upon the market and the valuer. It factors in macro and micro risk and the returns expectations of the industry.

Valuing a Warehouse:

Warehousing industry is in great demand in this pandemic situation. Therefore, it is very necessary to understand how to undertake the valuation of a Warehouse. The first thing we need to understand is the location of a Warehouse. Warehouses are located close to a port or any transport corridors. The Warehouses are located far from the City where the land cost is relatively low.

Due to this reason, we see a clustered development of Warehouses, for example – Warehouses in Bhiwandi, Panvel, Uran, etc. Because of these clusters, it is possible to value a warehouse by Direct Comparison Method as there would be transaction history and the market rates will be stable without any outliers.

For Example, Consider an Amazon Warehouse in Bhiwandi having a usable area of 2,00,000 sq. ft., RCC and MS Structure, 90 feet Height and is Built to Suit.

As shown in the above example, different aspects of the subject property are compared with its comparable. The important aspects to look for in a warehouse are its location, Useable Area, Height and type of Structure.

Attribute Ranking	Subject Property	Instance 1	Discount/Premium %	Comparable 2	Discount/Premium %
Name of the Property	Amazon Seller Services Private Limited	Hamilton Warehousing Private limited		The Universe Logidrome	
Location	Vashere Bhiwandi	Vashere biwandi	0.00%	Vashere biwandi	0.00%
Accessibility	Direct access to Kalyan-Sape road	Direct access to Kalyan-Sape road	0.00%	Direct access to Kalyan-Sape rd	-2.50%
Neighbourhood Profile	Immediate neighborhood includes warehouse	Immediate neighborhood includes wareho	0.00%	Immediate neighborhood inclu	0.00%
Type of Structure	RCC & MS strcuture	Pre Engineered Building	15.00%	Pre-Engineered Building	15.00%
Height	90 feet	50 feet	2.5%	49 feet	2.50%
Usable Area	2,00,000 sqft	1,00,000 sqft	2.50%	1,00,000 sqft	2.50%
Amenities	Excellent Amenities	Moderate Amenities	2.50%	Basic Amenities	2.50%
Built to suit	Yes	No	5.00%	No	5.00%
Stage of Construction	Operational	Operational	0.00%	Under Construction	5.00%
Type of Instance (Transacted / Quoted)		Transacted Q3, 2018	2.50%	Quoted Q1, 2019	-10.00%
Total Adjustment			30.00%		20.00%
Rate on usable area (INR psft)			2500		2900
Adjusted rate on usable area (INR psft)			3251		3480
Weightage			50.00%		50.00%
Acheivable rate on useable area (INR psft)					3,366
Acheivable rate on useable area (INR psft) - rounded off					3,400
Acheivable Market Value on usable area (INR)					96,66,94,800
Acheivable Market Value on usable area (INR) - rounded off					96,67,00,000

Premium and Discount are to be given based on the advantages or disadvantages of the properties over the Subject property.

Let's consider the height aspect in this scenario. The height of the subject property is higher than the others. It means that for the rate of the subject to be accurate, we have to increase the rate of the comparable by some factor to make the comparable similar to the subject property.

This is how Warehouse Valuation can be carried out to get a fair market Valuation of any said property.

6.5 Land

Land valuations are approached in two ways, sale comparison approach and land residual approach. In Sales comparison approach, land value is derived by comparing recent sales of a similar property. This is the most commonly used methods to estimate the value of the land. While going for this approach, one has to consider the sale adjustment grid. The sale adjustment grid means that while comparing, we have to make an adjustment like Non-market financing, change in market conditions (time), locational features, physical attributes, etc. The reason has to consider this adjustment is that every land parcel has its own merits and demerits.

Land Residual Approach, this method is used when the is a structure standing on the land parcel. In this method, the property is valued as if there was a building. Then the cost of developing the building is subtracted; the residual value is the land value.

An Example of Land Valuation

A land parcel of 5000 square feet is available for sale; the developer intends to develop an office building at a development cost of Rs.40 million.

	Amount	Size of Land	Date of transaction	Location Advantage
Parcel A	115000000	10000	20-08-2019	Inferior
Parcel B	1200000	1000	20-08-2019	Superior
Parcel C	24000000	2000	20-08-2018	Equal

A superior location will command a 5% premium whereas inferior location would command a 5% discount. A larger land parcel above 6000 sq. ft. will command Rs. 500 sq. ft. premium. The markets have depreciated by 5% year on year.

The above detail can be gathered through market research. We are going to use both methods Sale comparison and residual methods. We are going to give 50:50 weights for both the methods. In this example, we will take NOI (net operating income) of the building as 750000 per month and the cap rate to be taken as 9%. Again, this data can be calculated or gathered through market research.

	Rs/sqft	Market change	Plot size	Location	Adjusted Rs/sqft
Parcel A	₹ 11,500.00	₹ 10,925.00	₹ 500.00	₹ -575.00	₹ 10,850.00
Parcel B	₹ 11,200.00	₹ 10,640.00	₹ -	₹ 560.00	₹ 11,200.00
Parcel C	₹ 12,000.00	₹ 10,800.00	₹ -	₹ -	₹ 10,800.00
					₹ 10,950.00
			Value from Sale Comparison		₹ 5,47,50,000.00
			NOI per month		₹ 7,50,000.00
			NOI per annum		₹ 90,00,000.00
			Value of building @9% cap rate		₹ 10,00,00,000.00
			Cost		₹ 4,00,00,000.00
			Value from Residual approach		₹ 6,00,00,000.00
			Fair Value (Average)		₹ 5,73,75,000.00

Solution:

Value of the land is Rs. 5.73 Cr. In market change, we have taken depreciation as mentions above.

In this particular market land parcel, more than 6000 sq. ft. demands a premium of Rs. 500, so parcel A demands a premium.

Location is also considered, as we can see, we have adjusted for sale adjusted sale grid. As per the calculation, 5.47 Cr comes out based on sale comparison.

In the residual approach, we need to calculate the value of the entire property, and in this case, we have calculated based on the Cap rate method. To get the residual value, we have subtracted value of the building with the cost of building, so we get the value of land as 6 cr.

6.6 REIT

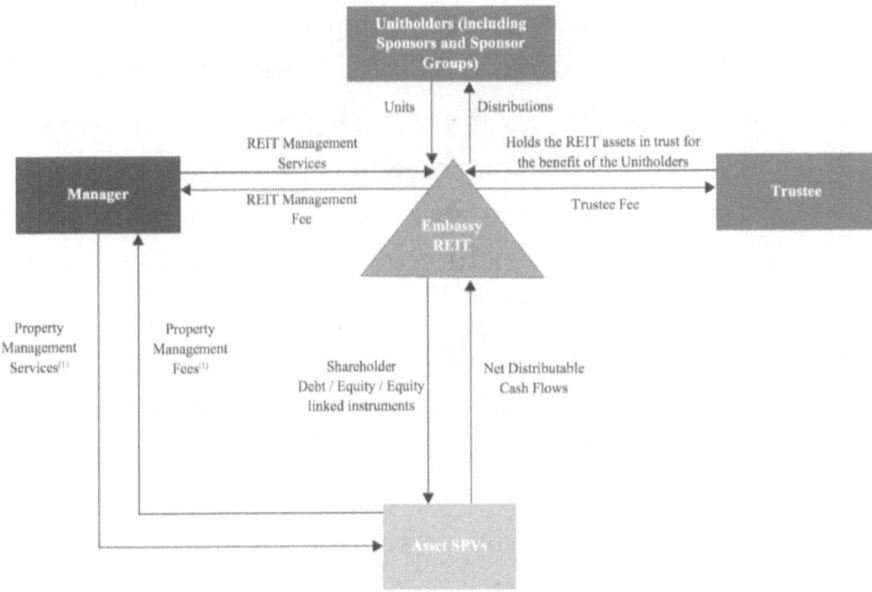

Figure 1 Structure of first REIT of India-Embassy

Real Estate Investment Trust (REIT) is a company or trust that owns, operates and finances a portfolio of income-generating real estate properties. The concept of REIT makes it possible for individual investors to invest a small amount in Real estate and earn dividends from them. The individual investors can reap the benefits of real estate investment without financing, managing, or buying any properties themselves.

The property valuation of the REIT portfolio is majorly approached with the DCF method of the Income approach. The steps adopted as part of the valuation are as follows:

1. *ASSET-SPECIFIC REVIEW:* Each asset's tenancy characteristics are reviewed separately as per their lease deeds and rent rolls. Title documents are reviewed for validation of ownership.

2. *MICRO-MARKET REVIEW:* A primary and secondary research is conducted in the catchment areas of respective assets to gauge similar properties' transaction activities. Surroundings and dynamics impacting the value of the property are considered. Historical leasings are also analysed.

3. *CASHFLOW PROJECTIONS:* The cashflows for operating and under-construction properties are considered separately. EBIDTA is utilized to arrive at the value of the property. Cashflow projections (10 years duration) are based on the existing lease.

4. The valuer follows the above steps to value each property in the REIT portfolio with Discounted Cashflow Methodology. The summation of all the properties' market value: operating & under-construction gives the market value of the REIT. The under-construction or partially constructed properties have higher discount rates as compared to the completed ones.

REPORT ON VALUATION

The purpose of the valuation report is to clearly and accurately lay down the conclusions of the property valuation. It must not be misleading or ambiguous and should refrain from creating a false impression. The valuer must use this report and draw attention and/ or comment on the issues that may affect the valuation's certainty or uncertainty.

A valuer is expected to visit the subject property and inspect it (preferably himself/herself). The visit is to observe and note relevant information with respect to structure, land, existing development in the surroundings, proximity to transport services, and available civic amenities. They must collect all the property's particulars and analyse the rules & regulations of local planning authorities. After considering everything, the valuer must prepare a thorough valuation report with suitable valuation technique.

As per RICS Red Book, the minimum matters that must be included in a valuation report are:

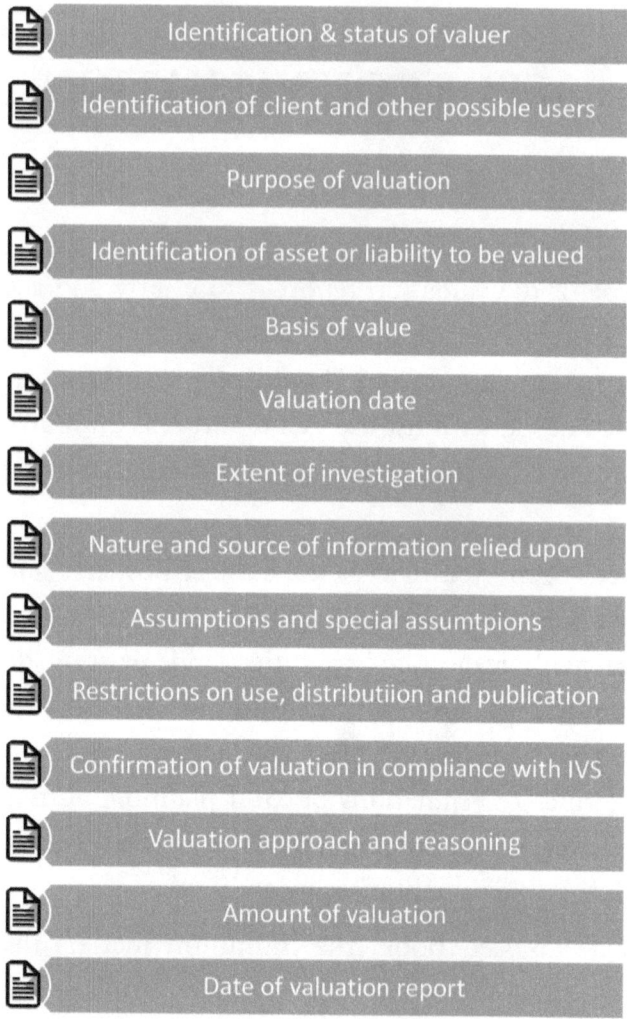

Identification & status of valuer

Identification of client and other possible users

Purpose of valuation

Identification of asset or liability to be valued

Basis of value

Valuation date

Extent of investigation

Nature and source of information relied upon

Assumptions and special assumtpions

Restrictions on use, distributiion and publication

Confirmation of valuation in compliance with IVS

Valuation approach and reasoning

Amount of valuation

Date of valuation report

However, the report's format and details are subjective and are in accordance with the terms of agreement of engagement between the valuer and client. If the client provides a specific list of requirements in the report, the valuer is expected to deliver a report that satisfies the checklist. In case of some alteration, the valuer must discuss the matter with the client in advance. The valuer must state reasons for any divergence from the minimum required matters needed to comply with requisite standards.

A common property valuation report can be broadly divided into the following parts:

7.1 Executive Summary

Ideally, a short but thorough summary of the entire valuation report is provided at the beginning of the report. It helps the reader to become acquainted with the entire content of the report quickly.

7.2 Valuation Report

This is the first part of the report after the executive summary. It lays a background for the valuation and explains the pre-process of conducting the valuation. The valuation report also brings a sense of transparency and trust between the valuer and the client. It may consist of following matters-

- Appointment: Declaration of the valuer being appointed by the client to carry out a valuation for the subject property.

- Conflicts of Interest: The valuer declares that the valuation was performed to advise the client without any bias or sense of personal gain/interest in the subject property.

- Scope of Work: To avoid any disagreements or confusion, the scope of work delivered to the client by the valuer is defined in clear terms as part of the final report.

- Purpose of Valuation: The valuation may be carried out to acquire the property, mortgage, insurance, taxation etc. The valuer is expected to define the purpose under this section of the report.

- Basis of Valuation: The valuer must specify the valuation methodology used for the subject property.

- Sources of Information: During the valuation, a valuer has to rely on various information sources available to him/her.

An extensive list of the sources is mentioned in the valuation report.

- Procedures performed: A brief of the process that a valuer went through to obtain a market value of the subject property.

- Limiting Conditions: It is imperative to lay down the limits with respect to the valuer, their process and the outcome achieved. This avoids any possible confusion between the valuer and the client.

- Disclosure in Publication: The valuer must define the permissible use of the contents of the report.

- Confidentiality: It is specified that the report contents are confidential for the addressee and for the purpose specified by them. The responsibility is not accepted by any other party for the entire content or part of it.

- Valuation: This part of the report declares that the valuation has been conducted according to the definition of Appraisal and Valuation Standards established by the RICS (RICS RED BOOK, 2020) and has been prepared by Valuers as defined by it.

7.3 Property Report

Thorough and extensive information about the subject property to be valued is a part of this section of the report. It consists of the following matters-

- Location: The site's location is defined along with the accessibility and transport services to the subject property.

- Property description: The valuer studies the subject property on their visit and mentions a detailed description. Property description includes infrastructure, services, ground conditions, environmental conditions, etc., of the subject property.

- Town planning and statutory conditions: The valuer analyses the subject property's land use as per the latest development plan. The impacts or effects of it may be considered in the valuation of the property.

- Approval status: The local authority's approval status for the plans of the subject property may be verified by the valuer. The valuer also considers the due charges or taxes paid/to be paid by the subject property authority.

- SWOT Analysis: The valuer must analyze the strengths, weakness, opportunities, and threats of the subject property.

7.4 Market Overview

The valuer provides a Real Estate market overview of the asset class relevant to the subject property. They show an analysis for the city economics and Real estate trends important for the valuation of the subject property. The valuer must also conduct a competition analysis in the area of the subject property.

7.5 Valuation Methodology and Commentary

A brief explanation of the valuation methodology applied by the valuer for the subject property is mentioned in the report. The valuer must also justify the choice of the method with an adequate and acceptable rationale. The valuer must also define the set of special assumptions used for the valuation of the subject property and mention a reliable basis for each one of them. The final market value derived from these assumptions and method is also mentioned in this part of the report.

SUSTAINABILITY EFFECTS ON VALUATION

Any property with 'sustainable' attributes is not a new property type, nor does it call for a deviation from the traditional valuation methods for the appraisal of income-producing properties. However, there can be numerous and significant differences between sustainable and traditional properties that appraisers must consider, research, and address.

Step 1: Identification of the Problem

In Step 1 of the valuation process, developing an understanding of the appraisal problem to be solved applies equally to sustainable and unsustainable valuation assignments. The identification of the appraisal problem involves the identification of the following: client; intended users of the appraisal; intended use of the appraisal; type of value, its definition, and the source of the definition; effective date of the opinion of value; relevant property characteristics for the property type, and intended use of the appraisal.

Step 2: Scope of Work Determination

Appraiser Competence

In addition to the standard issues of an appraiser's familiarity with the market area, property type, geographic area, intended use, specific laws and regulations, or analytical method, a property with sustainable aspects may require competence in a wide variety of additional areas.

Reliance on Reports of Others

Few appraisers are familiar with the detailed aspects of green building design, construction, operation, and maintenance. Therefore, in assessing a property's sustainable characteristics, most appraisers will utilize scientific and other technical evaluators or reports prepared by others, such as architects, engineers, and rating systems.

LEED litigation and Green Building Litigation

The last two decades have seen the increasingly rapid development of various green rating systems designed and marketed to measure the environmental impact of particular products and building design elements. Most green building programs share much in common with the two most well-known national green rating systems: the Leadership in Energy and Environmental Design (LEED) systems and the Green Globes program. Like rating systems for other products and processes, these building programs include some that are self-certifying and others that rely on a system of third-party verification.

Step 3: Data Collection and Property Description

Step 3 consists of collecting market area data, subject property data, and comparable property data.

Market Area Data

Data of particular relevance for a subject property with sustainable aspects is capturing the region, city, and neighbourhood's general characteristics as they may impact trends, overall supply, demand, and marketability.

Subject Property Data

The appraiser should consider the following sustainable characteristics. This is not an exhaustive list because assessing a property's sustainability characteristics is a complex activity wherein stakeholders may have different interpretations of sustainability, and the physical structures can be complex.

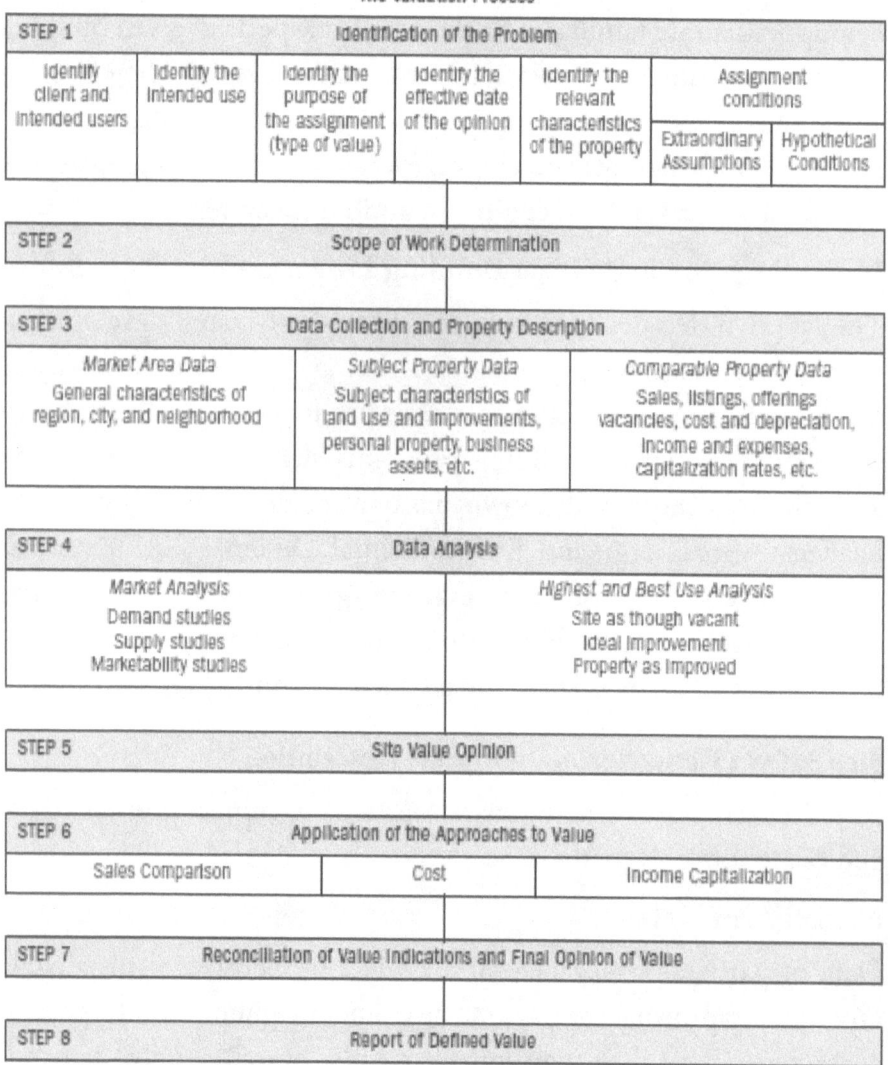

The Valuation Process

STEP 1	Identification of the Problem					
Identify client and intended users	Identify the intended use	Identify the purpose of the assignment (type of value)	Identify the effective date of the opinion	Identify the relevant characteristics of the property	Assignment conditions	
					Extraordinary Assumptions	Hypothetical Conditions

STEP 2	Scope of Work Determination

STEP 3	Data Collection and Property Description		
	Market Area Data	Subject Property Data	Comparable Property Data
	General characteristics of region, city, and neighborhood	Subject characteristics of land use and improvements, personal property, business assets, etc.	Sales, listings, offerings vacancies, cost and depreciation, income and expenses, capitalization rates, etc.

STEP 4	Data Analysis	
	Market Analysis	Highest and Best Use Analysis
	Demand studies Supply studies Marketability studies	Site as though vacant Ideal Improvement Property as Improved

STEP 5	Site Value Opinion

STEP 6	Application of the Approaches to Value		
	Sales Comparison	Cost	Income Capitalization

STEP 7	Reconciliation of Value Indications and Final Opinion of Value

STEP 8	Report of Defined Value

Building Materials

Where a building or its components are approaching the end of their economic life, any hazardous materials will impact the ability of the materials to be recycled or reused. This has a quantifiable impact on the cost of rehabilitation, demolition and land value.

The appraiser should seek expert opinions on potential hazards of building materials and cure, remediation and/or removal costs. The most common building material hazards are (1) respirable silica in sand, concrete, brick, Portland Cement, ceramic tile, stone, and other materials made of stone or earth; (2) lead in paint, plumbing, solder, connectors, roof flashings, and in fasteners; (3) asbestos in insulation, boilers, pipe covering, plaster, vinyl floor tile, glazing compound, caulking compound, roofing materials, drywall board and taping compound, linoleum, flooring, and other adhesives, acoustical materials, fireproofing insulation, and exterior siding materials; (4) polychlorinated biphenyls (PCBs) in electrical transformers, light fixture ballasts, and in other electrical equipment; (5) glass fibre in insulation and as reinforcement in plastics; (6) mineral wool in insulation and as reinforcement in vinyl composition floor tiles; (7) cadmium as a rust inhibitor on hardware and in paints; (8) asphalt as a sealant in adhesives and many roofing materials.

Location Analysis

The location analysis can consider its accessibility, contextual fit, and the impact of the site improvements on the subject site. To consistent with sustainability issues, the building may be accessible via a range of public and mass transportation for people and materials or more fuel-efficient or convenient transportation alternatives.

Resource Efficiency: Accomplished by utilizing materials that meet the following criteria:

a. Recycled Content: Products with identifiable recycled content, including post-industrial content with a preference for postconsumer content.

b. Natural, Plentiful or Renewable: Materials harvested from sustainably managed sources preferably have an independent certification (e.g., certified wood).

c. Resource-efficient Manufacturing Process: Products manufactured with resource-efficient processes including reduced energy consumption, minimizing waste (recycled, recyclable, and/or source reduced product packaging), and reducing greenhouse gases.

d. Locally Available: Building materials, components, and systems found locally or regionally saving energy and resources in transportation to the project site.

e. Salvaged, Refurbished, or Remanufactured: Includes saving material from disposal and renovating, repairing, restoring, or generally improving the appearance, performance, quality, functionality, or value of a product.

f. Reusable or Recyclable: Select materials that can be easily dismantled and reused or recycled at the end of their useful life.

g. Recycled or Recyclable Product Packaging: Products enclosed in recycled content or recyclable packaging.

h. Durable: Materials that are longer lasting or are comparable to Conventional products with long life expectancies.

Indoor Air Quality: Enhanced by utilizing materials that meet the following criteria:

a. Low or Non-toxic: Materials that emit few or no carcinogens, reproductive toxicants, or irritants, as demonstrated by the manufacturer.

b. Minimal Chemical Emissions: Products that have minimal emissions of Volatile Organic compounds (VOCs). Products that also maximize resource and energy efficiency while reducing chemical emissions.

c. Low-VOC Assembly: Materials installed with minimal VOC producing compounds, no-VOC mechanical attachment methods and minimal hazards.

d. Moisture Resistant: Products and systems that resist moisture or inhibit the growth of biological contaminants.

Energy Efficiency: Maximized by utilizing materials, components, and systems that help reduce energy consumption.

a. Water Conservation: Utilize materials and systems that help reduce water consumption in buildings and conserve water in landscaped areas.

b. Affordability: Consider when building product lifecycle costs are comparable to conventional materials, or as a whole, are within a project-defined percentage of the overall budget.

Income Capitalization

Sustainability Valuation Inputs for DCF. Consideration of sustainable aspects can be applied within the income approach. The discounted cash flow (DCF) method is addressed in this paper as the valuation-input parameters are explicit in this approach, whereas in the direct capitalization method, where they are mostly implicit, the analysis fails to capture the detailed sustainability-related income, expenses, and risks. In the DCF analysis, the main valuation-input variables are the risk premium in the capitalization and/or discount rates and the cash flow variables.

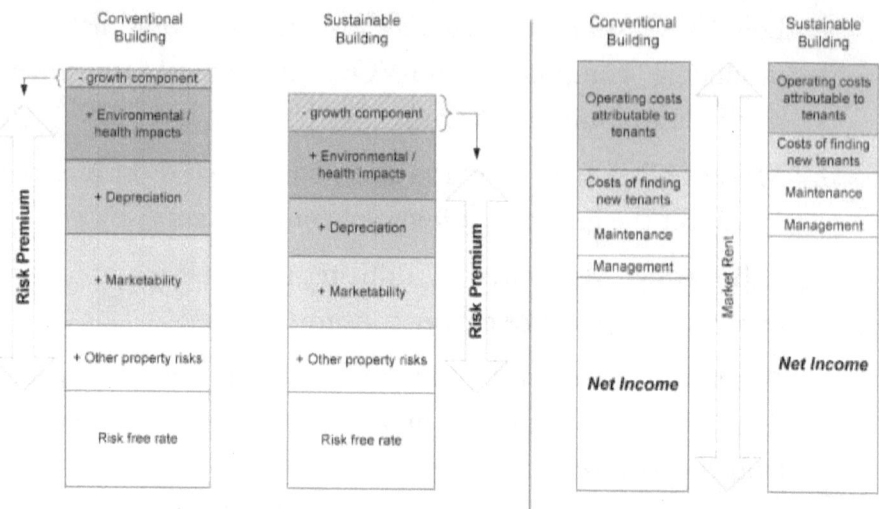

The DCF input variables for a property with sustainable aspects include many of the same inputs as a conventional building. However, the data, analysis, and final inputs must be based upon market-derived research of comparable sales and rentals of sustainable buildings with similar highest and best use, income expense ratios, future expectations of value changes over the projected holding period, risk characteristics, and other factors as determined by the appraiser.

This list of must-haves for the ideal comparable and market-derived input variables is most appropriate for the classroom, although seldom within the appraisal office's reality. Quantitative analyses of data and information on comparable properties will likely indicate a numerical range for each valuation-input variable for the foreseeable future. The practitioner's qualitative judgment will ultimately determine the final value of key input parameters.

LITERATURE REVIEW AND CASE STUDY

Factors affecting Urban Land Value in Indian Cities – Chennai City as A Case Study Volume I, Issue III, August 2014, IJRSI, ISSN 2321-2705

Santhakumar Swamidurai, Assistant Professor, Anna University, Chennai, India

The increasing land prices have brought immense pressure for development in most Indian cities within the city limits and its agglomeration areas. The increase in value is found mainly along major economic growth corridors which will further inevitability increase the land price in core areas of the city. Chennai, the fourth most densely populated Indian city, is undergoing this intense pressure for development in housing, industrial and commercial sectors. The land value is broadly dependent on the economy, urban sprawl, location, land use, infrastructure availability and land scarcity in the city. The research analyses all factors affecting land value in the city.

Evaluation of slum improvements, 1996 – A case study in Visakhapatnam, India

Peter Abelson Department of Economics, Macquarie University, Sydney, NSW2109, Australia

The paper explores how to determine initiatives for slum development and highlights the debate in Visakhapatnam, India, with a case study of developments in 170 slums. The valuation methods discussed involve land and house prices, cost-effectiveness, contingent valuation, changes in revenue and changes in values. The paper reports assessments of the slum development programme as a total in Visakhapatnam, progress in 19 sample slums, and investment in health care, schools and technical training relying mainly on property prices but also on other valuation methods. The return on the whole programme was marginal, as determined by the willingness to pay value. The findings are subject to assumptions regarding spending on recurring maintenance. Important economies of scale showed investment returns in individual slums, with better returns in bigger slums. Training gains were high in sales, and the educational courses were likely justified on the ability to pay grounds. However, the condition of health status improvement was seen. The paper concludes that the ability to pay valuations will usefully contribute to programme assessments, despite government efforts to direct assistance to poor areas. Finally, the paper provided alternative areas of study that would help in improving the procedures for evaluation.

Defining the fair market value of land in a thin land market of India to pay just compensation – a case study

Tapas Roy, R. Jayaraj and Anil Kumar, Published online 4 April 2017

India has a fresh LARR 2013 Land Acquisition Act. Its content varies substantially from that of its previous LAA 1894 edition. However, the Act tends to treat the adjacent lands' average market valuation as the plot's equal market valuation and avoids the disappearance of an active land market in India. In India, land plots are limited, and ownership is divided. Smaller land plots differ in their qualitative characteristics and therefore, in their values. Sales information is scarce because of the thin market and cannot be used for averaging directly. To prevent criticism of paying little to landowners, the act raised the solatium to two to four times the average market valuation. This paper suggests the use of a rational computing approach for the land valuation to pay only compensation. This involves the detection of attributes influencing the price of agricultural land and the use of differential attributes to change, before averaging sales prices. To get the fair market valuation, adjusted selling prices can then be averaged and used to pay only.

The Valuation of Holiday Hotels. A Case Study of Negril, Jamaica
Tina Beale, 2014

Globally, climate change has contributed to many catastrophic consequences. The alarming rates at which the island's shorelines recede are one influence that has changed Jamaica's hotel industry. This paper describes a study on receding shorelines in the third-largest tourist centre in Jamaica and suggests a method for the valuation of vacation hotels in Negril, Jamaica, called Discounted Cash Flow (DCF). The study provides important points against the use when valuing hotels of the Earnings, Revenue Equivalent and Contractors Methods of Valuation. The article argues that the study of the DCF is the best way to provide the valuation for holiday hotels, while professionals and scholars have argued that it offers, at best, the value of the investment value.

ADDITIONAL CHARACTERISTICS THAT AFFECT THE VALUATION

For real estate, which is definitely on the rise, statistics show property valuation corrections are taking a turn for the better. Real estate prices and their valuation is affected by multiple factors other than the primitive considerations, in more defined and elaborate ways.

Interest rates, demographics, state of the economy, time of purchase/valuation, price escalations, recessions in the market, sustainability, ease of living and design, etc. are various factors that affect valuation in the current scenario along with the traditional aspects of location, amenities and futuristic infrastructure development.

List of additional characteristics that affect a property valuation:

a. **Disposable income:**

    Valuation of property is directly related to the chunk of disposable in the purchaser's hands or the majority of the residing population in the area. Thus, properties near IT hubs, service sector, etc. are valuated at a higher price than those near agricultural or industrial areas.

b. **Demand and supply:**

    Demand and supply for a particular product is the major driver of valuation and pricing. As the supply or availability of real estate decreases the valuation increases.

    For example, because of the boon in the affordable segment and many developers coming with majorly 1 and

2 BHK configurations, the 3 and 4 BHK configuration supply reduced at multiple locations. Thus, leading to the increase in the premium over the larger inventory at various locations with demand for larger carpet areas.

c. **Design and structural aspects:**

As customers are becoming more particular about the property and the ease that comes with it, sellers are charging a heavy premium for grade A residential and commercial structures. For example, mivan or aluminium shuttering construction would charge a premium over conventional construction. Other than the type of structure and foundation, advanced design considerations are gaining importance. Resilient designs, smart and flexible user-friendly layouts with minimum wastage of area, safety considerations, durability, physical attributes such as specifications and quality of materials, floor to floor height, waterproofing, and external appearance of the structure, etc. are all taken into consideration while evaluating a property.

For example, commercial spaces that comply with social distancing norms such as larger area per person, minimum and smart common areas will add safety premiums. While in residential, considerations such as common areas for each floor or group of floors to cater to social distancing norms and strict facility management considerations to look after sanitization and safety would add to premiums. Also, properties with automation and customizable options further shoot up the premiums in real estate.

In conclusion, Before deciding on any real estate, an individual should perform a thorough analysis of all the factors affecting the property's valuation. This homework and investigation will ensure easy liquidity, more lucrative investments, and better returns.

These factors play an important role in determining the value of a property, but there are also other complex reasons that come into play. Even though many of these stated factors indicate a direct relationship between the factor and the value, the outcome can be different in reality. However, understanding the factors that affect the property value is essential for conducting a valuation.

www.ingramcontent.com/pod-product-compliance
Lightning Source LLC
Chambersburg PA
CBHW021005180526
45163CB00005B/1901